STUFF KIDS SHOULD KNOW

STUFF KIDS SHOULD KNOW

THE MIND-BLOWING HISTORIES OF (ALMOST) EVERYTHING

CHUCK BRYANT AND **JOSH CLARK;**
CONTRIBUTION BY **NILS PARKER**

Henry Holt and Company
New York

Henry Holt and Company, *Publishers since 1866*
Henry Holt® is a registered trademark of Macmillan Publishing Group, LLC
120 Broadway, New York, NY 10271 • mackids.com

Our books may be purchased in bulk for promotional, educational, or business use. Please
contact your local bookseller or the Macmillan Corporate and Premium Sales Department at
(800) 221-7945 ext. 5442 or by email at MacmillanSpecialMarkets@macmillan.com.

Library of Congress Control Number: 2022920246

First edition, 2023
Book design by Maria Williams
Printed in the United States of America by BVG, Fairfield, Pennsylvania

ISBN 978-1-250-62244-0
10 9 8 7 6 5 4 3 2 1

*For my daughter, Ruby, whose endless curiosity
continues to inspire my own.* —C. B.

*For Umi and Momo, the two best things that ever
happened to me* —J. C.

CONTENTS

PREFACE

Hey, and welcome to the book, everybody. We're Josh Clark and Charles W. "Chuck" Bryant. And this is a totally mind-blowing and incomplete compendium of mostly interesting but, more important, completely random topics that span from Mr. Potato Head to demolition derbies.

Here's the first interesting thing: We've been podcasting since 2008, and we've talked about writing an *SYSK*[1] book for a long time now, but we thought it would never happen and we kind of stopped thinking about it, so we're just tickled that it finally came together, and that we are able to offer a young reader's edition of it.

Actually, we're not exactly sure what's interesting about that little bit of personal trivia, to be honest. We know there's got to be something, though, because we feel like there's something interesting about everything.

Understanding this idea—that there's something interesting about everything—is one of the core beliefs of the entire *Stuff You Should Know* universe, and this book is no exception. It has had a profound effect on us as podcasters, as writers, and as humans in the world. And it has informed

---

[1] Short for *Stuff You Should Know*, the totally awesome name of our totally awesome pod.

everything we do, most directly by supercharging a very specific trait we both possess: curiosity.

The belief that there is something interesting about everything has opened our eyes, our ears, and our minds to the world around us in ways we never could have expected. From the odd to the mundane, from the overlooked to the underappreciated, from the infinite to the infinitesimal; whether it involved a person, place, or thing, whether it was an idea or an event, a process or a system, real or imagined, every day we found something that made us sit up, take notice, and say, "Huh, *that's* interesting . . . we should talk about that."[2]

Fifteen years and over a thousand podcast episodes later, we decided to take the same approach with a book: Josh picks some random topics that we've been curious about recently, and Chuck picks a bunch of others; we'll see what kind of interesting stuff we can find, and then write about it. And we did. And it was awesome. But it was mostly old farts who read that book. What about all those younger brains just begging to get in on all these interesting things? We couldn't leave them hanging, so we wrote another book. *This* book.

The results, if you are a fan of the show already, will hopefully feel familiar. That was the idea, at least. There's lots of stuff you should know; there's some weirdness and some humor; there are some counterintuitive explanations, some unexpected realizations, some accidental puns, more than a few awesome band names, a heaping helping of dad

....

[2] And in a few cases, when we really had to dig, we said, "We *will* find what's interesting about this."

2

jokes, tons of dives down little rabbit holes,[3] and several illustrations by an artist named Carly Monardo that we are totally in love with (the illustrations, not Carly, though she is wonderful and makes awesome comics).

We also worked with a co-writer, a great guy named Nils Parker, who helped us tremendously with research, writing, and generally guided us through what's what with publishing a book. Having a hired gun to help us out was a tough pill to swallow at first, both of us being writers, but as the book project unfolded in earnest, all of our illusions (delusions, really) quickly fell away and we were grateful for Nils's help right out of the gate. Had he not been around, you might be picking up this book in 2050 rather than 2023. Nils has gotten the *SYSK* vibe so thoroughly that he's become as much a part of the *SYSK* gang as Jeri and Frank the Chair, so be sure to add him to your holiday card list.

Together we honed this book into a sword of wisdom for you to wield between games or at birthday parties, anywhere you feel like impressing people. Use it wisely. Oh, and it just so happens that the sword analogy is also a really great segue for our next point.

In *The Book of Five Rings*, the seventeenth-century samurai Miyamoto Musashi wrote, "From one thing, know ten thousand things." Musashi was a master swordsman and he knew that discipline fully. But he didn't *only* know that. He also learned metallurgy to understand how to make the

---

[3] They take the form of footnotes . . . like this one. Think of them as Easter eggs.

3

strongest sword; physiology and anatomy to understand the physical vulnerabilities of his opponents; human psychology to understand their mental vulnerabilities; geometry to understand angles of attack; and physics to understand leverage. The list almost certainly goes on.[4]

What Musashi was saying is that if you master one thing completely, it will teach you about so many other things in the process. And while we agree with the great samurai and are very grateful that we never faced the slashing end of his fury, we have respectfully chosen to take the opposite approach to knowledge. From the very beginning of *Stuff You Should Know*, we've learned that from ten thousand things (or in this case, fourteen things), you can know one thing. And that is, when you look closely enough, everything is connected, one way or another.[5]

Just as with everything else in the world, there is a deep interconnectedness to the randomness within the fourteen chapters of this book.

You can read it front to back, back to front, or jump around;[6] whichever reading adventure you choose, what you will find are connection points and narrative threads that join them.

....

[4] Gee, his teachers must be proud.

[5] This is, of course, the whole premise of the Six Degrees of Kevin Bacon game. That guy has been in so many films everybody in Hollywood can surely be linked to him within six connections. The game alone gives the Great Interconnectedness of All Things an important purpose.

[6] You can also jump up, jump up, and get down or jump, jump if you like. Kind of crazy how in one year, two hip-hop groups, House of Pain and Kris Kross, both had jumpy songs hit the top ten. Even crazier—Chris Kelly and Chris Smith of Kris Kross were only 12 and 13 years old!

The first thing you'll notice is the first thing we noticed: just how many podcast episodes we've done related to topics that we only touch on in each chapter. These connections back to the show are noted with lists to specific episodes that were referenced for the material in each chapter.

What you might then notice is how wide and far these connections go. We go back in time millions of years with prehistoric wildebeests and elephants to learn about water-dowsing. We travel trillions of miles into space to better grasp the magnitude and proportion of massive personal wealth. We travel the globe to meet common criminals in Britain, artificially aged mice at Harvard University, and a guy who wandered around Malaysia. You've got in your hands a guided tour of interconnected time and space, and all for a pretty fair price when you consider it like that.

Our hope is that in reading this book you feel more connected to the world around you: to the person next to you on the train and the stranger on the opposite side of the world, to the beginning of human history and to the ends of eras you weren't alive for, to places you may never go and people you will probably never meet. More than anything, we hope you learn some new stuff along the way. That would be pretty cool too.

Okay, well, that's probably enough setup. Let's start the book already!

JOSH CLARK & CHUCK BRYANT

CHAPTER 1

MR. POTATO HEAD

AMERICA'S TOY

We love toys. New toys, old toys, big toys, small toys.[7] Toys that need batteries, toys that only require your imagination. It doesn't matter to us. We love toys the way milk loves cookies.

We talk to each other about toys more than any other topic besides maybe those Nazi jerks and earth science.

So far, we've done episodes on Etch A Sketch, Silly Putty, Play-Doh, action figures, Slinky, Barbie®, Rubik's Cube, Easy-Bake Ovens, *E.T.* the video game, and probably a whole lot of others we're forgetting right now. Like sugary cereal and puppies, even when a toy is bad, it's still great. Yet somehow, we have never talked about Mr. Potato Head.[8]

....

[7] See especially: our long-standing Great G.I. Joe Size Debate in Chapter 6.

[8] For reasons that remain unclear, articles about Mr. Potato Head are riper for wordplay than naming a boat. So, unlike the authors of nearly every Mr. Potato Head profile we read in preparation for this chapter, we are going to do our very best not to make any potato-based puns. Wish us luck.

Those of us who were raised in the United States are all probably familiar with the same basic version of Mr. Potato Head: the smiling, quasi-legless russet potato that, when fully assembled, looks like a teacher who thinks his cheesy smile will convince you to like taking tests.

But he didn't always look like that. For the first decade or so of his life, Mr. Potato Head wasn't even really a potato. He was barely even a mister.

He was an oddly configured, 30-piece "funny face man" kit that cost 98 cents and required buyers to provide their own potato—an *actual* potato—to use as the head. Potato in hand, a 1950s kid could attach said funny face and build said man.

THE ORIGINAL MR. POTATO HEAD PART LIST		
OF COURSE THAT'S IN THERE	OKAY, WELL, THAT'S INTERESTING	WAIT, AM I MISSING SOMETHING?
Eyes (2 pairs)	Hats (3)	
Ears	Eyeglasses	
Nose (4)	Tobacco Pipe	
Mouth (2)	Facial Hair (81)	Yeah . . . A Friggin' Head!
Hands		
Feet		
Body		

And if they didn't have a potato? Not to worry: "ANY FRUIT OR VEGETABLE MAKES A FUNNY FACE MAN."

Or so said the manufacturer, Hassenfeld Bros Inc., who printed those words on the top of every Mr. Potato Head box as a way to market the toy's versatility.

It worked too. The Rhode Island–based company sold more than a million units their first full year in production, making it Hassenfeld Bros' first major success in the toy business. Eventually they condensed their name and became Hasbro—the largest toymaker in the world. And we can assume the potato farmers of America appreciated their efforts.

This very food-focused approach might have been the end of the brothers if they had gone for it only a few years earlier. It nearly proved to be for Mr. Potato Head's inventor, George Lerner, when he first went out looking for a buyer. Lerner originally called his invention "Funny Face Man"— thus the tagline on the side of the original Mr. Potato Head box—and spent the better part of the next three years struggling to gin up interest from toy companies. This proved to be a Herculean task because, at that time, the average American looked at using a potato for a toy as a shameful waste of food.

It's weird to think of a world where Mr. Potato Head never existed, because you could make a pretty strong case that Mr. Potato Head is *the* toy of the American century. In fact, we'll just say it: Mr. Potato Head is *the* toy of the American century.[9] That's right. A legless potato person, who started

----

[9] The "American century" started way back at the end of World War II, so just relax, all you SpongeBob and Pokémon fans.

out as plastic parts with pins for kids to stab into an actual potato, isn't just some disposable, forgettable distraction. It turns out he is a reflection of America's recent history and culture. As Mr. Potato Head went, so went the country (or vice versa, but let's not split hairs). You could even say Mr. Potato Head *is* America.

Our theory might sound a little half-baked,[10] but the timeline of events says otherwise. Get a load of this:

1949

George Lerner invents "Funny Face Man" and it nearly dies on the vine because people are still worried about the availability of food. Keep in mind, this is only four years after the end of World War II. Food rationing is still fresh in their minds. This is also the year the Cold War really kicks into gear.[11]

It is true that the United States *did* win World War II and that life in America is good by this time, but it isn't "turn your root vegetables into toys" good. If an adult is going to give a potato to their child in 1949, it's going in that child's mouth, not in their toy box.

....

[10] This was an unintentional pun and we fought bitterly with the publishers to have it removed. We lost.

[11] Sure, the US and Soviet Union banded together to whup the Nazis in 1945, but no one said they liked each other. No matter the topic— nuclear weapons, spy skills, athletes, space rockets—for 40 years they spent all their energy trying to one-up the other. Now we call it the Cold War.

1951

Lerner finally finds a buyer: a cereal company that wants to give the "funny face" kits away as prizes in their boxes of cereal. And, really, who doesn't look at a box of yummy breakfast cereal and think "I want to play with a potato!"?

But before the cereal company can put any prize-filled boxes on store shelves, Lerner meets with the Hassenfeld brothers up in Pawtucket, Rhode Island. The Hassenfelds had made all their money to this point by producing things like pencil cases and toy medical kits that let kids play doctor. They see the fun in this "Funny Face Man," so they buy the idea back from the cereal company, rename it Mr. Potato Head, and give George Lerner a cut of every sale.

1952

Now things really start to shift. Television begins to invade American homes. Just three years earlier, fewer than half a million television sets were purchased. But by the end of 1952, 26 million homes have a TV. And they couldn't have come at a better time either. This year the polio outbreak is the worst in America's history, driving most kids indoors, particularly during summer, when polio is thought to be most vicious.[12]

....

[12] Polio is a virus that attacks cells in the central nervous system, killing them off and sometimes causing paralysis. Kids caught it from swimming in contaminated water. When outbreaks began, terrified parents put their kids on lockdown. Today in the US, polio has been almost entirely eliminated thanks to vaccination.

Remember, they had no internet back then. Recognizing an opportunity, Hassenfeld Brothers decides to run TV ads for Mr. Potato Head. Not only is Mr. Potato Head the very first toy to be advertised on TV, the Hassenfelds pioneered a new advertising strategy: advertise directly to children, urging them to beg their parents to buy the toy. Today this strategy is so widespread it has its own name: "nag factor."[13]

1953

The Hassenfeld brothers decide that Mr. Potato Head needs to settle down. So he marries Mrs. Potato Head and they honeymoon in Boise, Idaho (which, for potatoes, is like Disney World and Disneyland mashed into one).[14] It's not long before they set down roots and have a couple of kids, a boy and a girl named Spud and Yam. It's a fitting, starchy, all-American choice for two reasons: 1) We're smack in the middle of the Baby Boom,[15] and 2) America's new favorite toy couple now mirrors America's favorite TV couple, Lucy and Ricky Ricardo, who start the year by having a baby in

....

[13] In the UK, it's called "pester power." Even their term for being annoying sounds more refined.

[14] That pun thing happened again!

[15] When every Tom, Dick, and Harry (yes, those names were common in the '50s) returned from World War II, they went back to work in the factories and making babies.

an episode of *I Love Lucy.* The episode is watched by nearly three quarters of all homes that have TVs.[16]

EARLY 1960s

Eventually the 1960s arrive, as most people expected them to. It is a decade defined, at least in part, by terms like "consumerism," "materialism," and "conspicuous consumption," which is technical talk for people wanting more, more, MORE!

....

[16] In an amazing life-imitating-art moment, the episode filmed in the fall of 1952 airs the same day (January 19, 1953) that Lucille Ball gives birth to her second child in real life—this one a boy, named Desi Arnaz Jr., after his father and Lucy's co-star, whose real name is Desi Arnaz III, which actually makes their son Desi Arnaz IV. So that's not confusing at all.

And what are Mr. and Mrs. Potato Head doing? We presume they're buying lots of *stuff*, just like every other upwardly mobile middle-class American family. They buy a boat. Then a plane, a train, and an automobile. It's like something out of a movie![17]

MID-TO-LATE 1960s

It takes twelve years, but Hasbro finally leaves behind its bonehead "no potato head in the Mr. Potato Head box" policy and starts producing separate plastic heads and bodies with prefab holes for the parts. It's the first step toward the Mr. Potato Head we know today.

The decision to move toward plastic is due partly to complaints—go figure, parents were tired of finding moldy potatoes under sofas—and partly to injuries. Itty-bitty body parts and sharp pins aren't exactly toddler-proof![18] So Hasbro solves both problems with one word: plastics.

1970s

By the time the '70s roll around and things get truly groovy, Congress passes the Child Protection Act of 1966, and the Child Protection and Toy Safety Act in 1969 (aka the Summer of Love and Child Safety). These new laws mean

....

[17] Specifically, *Planes, Trains & Automobiles*.

[18] During this era, it finally dawned on someone that you could make things safer. Seat belts in cars weren't even mandatory until 1968.

Hasbro has to combine the separate body and head pieces of Mr. Potato Head into one single, large body. This new version will be impossible for a small child to swallow unless that child can stretch their jaw like a reticulated python.[19]

Unfortunately, this is Hasbro's first crack at a combined body form, and they kinda screw it up big-time. This bulbous version looks more like someone took a butternut squash and charred it in a campfire. In other words, not good.

To make matters worse, they replace all the holes in the body with tabbed slots that only accept the pieces that belong in those specific spots: the mouth where the mouth goes, the ears where the ears go, and so on. What fun is that? Mr. Potato Head is now the world's easiest, creepiest puzzle. Oh, and they forgot to give him arms.

The '70s are clearly rough for Mr. Potato Head.

1980s–1990s

The next thirty years bring the reign of the Mr. Potato Head we all know and love. It's the version of Mr. Potato Head who bypasses all other toys and begins to participate in, and affect, culture itself. He gets into politics and activism. On top of that, he achieves every potato's Holy Grail: his very own video game.[20]

....

[19] Forget the myths, snakes can't *unhinge* their jaws. A 23-foot reticulated python did, however, *stretch* its jaws wide enough to swallow a human.

[20] Sure, it's for preschoolers and required one of those old-fashioned CD-ROM thingies, but, hey, you get to lasso clouds.

In 1985, Mr. Potato Head returns to Boise, where he and the missus honeymooned all those years ago. He runs for mayor. Two years later, in 1987, he participates in the American Cancer Association's Eleventh Great American Smokeout and agrees to quit smoking for good. He hands over his pipe to none other than C. Everett Koop, the US Surgeon General with the greatest Chin Curtain of all time (more on Chin Curtains in Chapter 4), in the hopes of inspiring others to quit. As far as we know, he has not relapsed.

In the '90s, Mr. and Mrs. Potato Head sponsor the League of Women Voters' "Get Out the Vote" campaign. At the same time, Mr. Potato Head continues his health kick. In an attempt to inspire couch potatoes, he accepts an award from one of the world's best bodybuilders (and the chairman of the President's Council on Physical Fitness and Sports)— Arnold Schwarzenegger—in a ceremony on the White House lawn.

PRESENT-DAY POTATO

If, by now, Mr. Potato Head isn't forever cemented as a pop culture icon, his role in the *Toy Story* films, beginning in 1995, does the trick. Of all the toys in the movies, he is the one who is the most immediately recognizable and the least changed—since the 1970s, anyway. If three generations of family sat down tomorrow to watch *Toy Story* for the first time, all three would probably be like, "Aww, Mr. Potato Head!"

By that very fact, our theory that Mr. Potato Head is the toy of the American century remains sound.

The *New York Times* writer N. R. Kleinfeld hit the nail on the head when he wrote back in 1987 that "Hasbro was one of the first companies to recognize the value in endowing a toy with a fantasy life, a practice that has become increasingly commonplace." Mr. Potato Head was first and is still the best at it.

Just consider how often we use the words *he* and *his* in this chapter. You don't have to actually count, we can just tell you, it's a lot.[21] And we're not alone. Almost everyone who has ever written about Mr. Potato Head has called him, well, a *him* and not an *it*.[22]

We don't think about Mr. Potato Head as an object the way we do other toys. We anthropomorphize him, treating him like a person. That's because an entire generation grew up with him on their TVs and in their living rooms. The Baby Boomer generation and Mr. Potato Head basically came of age together. And as the Baby Boomers got older, raised families, started running companies and cities, and began making decisions that affected millions of people, Mr. Potato Head always seemed to be right there, first as a reflection of the times, then as a player in the changing of the times. Just look at where he's shown up in modern

....

[21] Let's just keep it at that, shall we?

[22] However, you might start reading "they." In 2021, Hasbro dropped the "Mr." and rebranded to the gender-neutral "Potato Head."

times, dressing up like various members of the Star Wars and Marvel universes[23]—two of the most popular and profitable franchises in film history.

When you sit back and think about Mr. Potato Head, it's hard not to smile at least a little bit. And if you're like Mr. Potato Head, you can put that smile almost anywhere you please.[24]

....

[23] If you don't own Darth Tater or the full collection of Agents of S.P.U.D., then you're not doing fun right.

[24] Mr. Potato Head can put his smile and every other body part in a storage compartment right where his butt would be. Do NOT try that at home!

~~~~~~

CHAPTER 2

HOW TO GET LOST

AND SEVEN WAYS TO STAY LIKE THAT

Do you want to hear an astounding number? 65,439. Sure, it's not so astounding on its own, so you have to know the context: That's the number of search and rescue (SAR)[25] missions launched for people who went missing inside America's national parks between 1992 and 2007.

65,439! That's basically the entire population of a city like Jupiter, Florida.[26] Over a fifteen-year period, that's nearly twelve lost people per day.

One person every two hours who just went *poof* and disappeared into the wilderness somewhere across America. Like

....

[25] We have done not one but two episodes on SAR, one of them just on SAR dogs.

[26] As of 2020, with a population of 65,791 that includes Michael Jordan and Tiger Woods, Jupiter is precisely the 570th largest city in the United States. Even more interesting than that is the fact that there are 569 cities in America with more than a football stadium's worth of people (that's roughly anywhere between 60,000 to 80,000) living in them.

we said, astounding. Fortunately, the period of time people are typically lost for is rarely ever very long. The average search and rescue mission for a lost hiker or hunter—who make up nearly 50 percent of those national parks cases—lasts about ten hours, which usually isn't a life-threatening amount of time, although it's probably several hours longer than it takes to scare the bejesus out of them.

Interestingly, 2007 marks the beginning of a significant downward trend in missing persons reports. What happened? It wasn't a country-wide rise in Eagle Scouts or the long-term impact of *Dora the Explorer* finally kicking in. It was smartphones. It just so happens that 2007 was the year the first iPhone came out, and it had onboard SMS and map software and internet. The next year, Apple added GPS to the phone, which made tracking people easier and getting lost much harder. With a computer in your pocket that doubles as a satellite beacon and telephone, you almost have to *try* to get lost.

Which, of course, people still did.

Thousands of people around the world continue to get lost every day, and for all sorts of reasons: They get caught in difficult terrain or the weather suddenly turns sour on them; they don't pay enough attention to where they're going (or where they've been); they get separated from their group or their battery goes dead. Sometimes darkness falls and obscures the path, which must be awfully spooky; other times they simply get turned around in a giant mall, or make too many wrong turns in a big city where they don't speak the language.[27] And then there is the age-old problem of getting lost while you're running away from a serial killer at an overly wooded summer camp with no idea what direction leads to town.

There are a million different ways to get lost, but what's interesting is that when people get lost (particularly out in nature), they all act in the exact same ways. This is the discovery of psychology professor Kenneth Hill, PhD, who studies the psychology of being lost at Saint Mary's University

---

[27] That was pretty jarring, huh? In your mind's eye you'd been imagining yourself lost in the woods, in the rain, in the dark, without a map, then suddenly—BAM!—you're in a big city like Jakarta or Casablanca where you don't speak the language, lost as ever. What a ride.

way up in Nova Scotia, Canada.[28] Independent of race or gender or nationality or outdoor experience or even age, when people get lost, they kind of lose their minds—but in predictable ways. They forget their training (if they had any).

They forget what they were taught by parents and teachers—some forget themselves entirely and go a little berserk. And they engage in some combination of the same eight behaviors, kind of like robots that have been programmed with outdated guidance software that's chock-full of bugs:[29]

RANDOM TRAVELING   ROUTE TRAVELING
DIRECTION TRAVELING   ROUTE SAMPLING
DIRECTION SAMPLING   VIEW ENHANCING
BACKTRACKING   STAYING PUT

The thing is: When you take a closer look at each of these "lost person behaviors," as they're called in the search and rescue field, it's easy to see how each one of us could fall prey to them. Including you—yes, you!—and everyone you know and love. All of you: lost, lost, lost!

RANDOM TRAVELING

Lost person behavior seems to start here, and it works just the way it sounds: You move around in all sorts of random

....

[28] Or, if you live in Nova Scotia, "here."

[29] It's not a bug, it's a feature.

directions, hoping to find your way out. The irony is that it's usually unconscious random traveling that gets you lost in the first place, which then triggers even more random traveling that gets you even more lost. As Dr. Hill explains it, this is because most people experience "high emotional arousal" once they realize they don't know where they are, and so they start following "the path of least resistance, with no apparent purpose other than to find something or some place that looks familiar." (This is a very calm, Canadian way of saying that when people realize they're lost they "totally freak out and run around like a chicken with its head cut off."[30])

Eventually, though, the adrenaline dump subsides, and the poor lost person starts to behave with a little more purpose and sense. They focus on traveling specific routes and directions, instead of letting the panic of having no idea where they are guide them like the world's worst back seat driver.

ROUTE TRAVELING

This is one of the first strategies people employ after freaking out. They spot an animal trail, or a dry streambed,[31] or a ridgeline, or what they think is a path, maybe, somewhere

---

[30] What, you don't know about the Mike the Headless Chicken Festival? Quick, head to Fruita, Colorado, and don't miss the PEEPS® eating contest!

[31] Also known as an "arroyo," "ditch," "gully," or "wash"—is it weird that there are so many words for "a place where there used to be running water"?

23

in the distance, and they follow it regardless of whether or not they know what direction it's going in. The hope is that eventually they'll stumble across something they recognize. The *theory*, we guess, is that if all roads lead to Rome, and there are a thousand roads to Mecca, at least one of these routes should lead to the trailhead where their car is parked. Except usually that's not the case. To make matters worse, once the route dead-ends, they almost never try to backtrack. Instead they either revert to random traveling (especially if they're younger) or they pick a direction and go.

DIRECTION **TRAVELING**

According to Dr. Hill, picking a cardinal direction and heading that way is a really bad strategy. That's unfortunate, because this is the one that often gets employed by overconfident outdoor enthusiasts and takes them from really lost to *totally* lost in very short order, because travel is no longer about hooking up to a trail or identifying landmarks, but simply going in whatever direction the lost person has chosen. Under normal circumstances that doesn't make sense. It doesn't make sense under lost circumstances either. There are even stories of hunters and hikers ignoring trails and roads, "cross[ing] power lines, highways and even backyards" because they're convinced those landmarks (which generally point in the direction of civilization) are going the wrong way, while they themselves are headed in the "right" direction. *Backyards*. There does not seem to be an instinct to backtrack on the part of direction travelers either—which is really something for a seasoned nature lover, because if there's one strategy you'd think they would be best suited to for getting *un*-lost, it's backtracking. But no (or "non," if you happen to be lost in France).

BACKTRACKING

As you might expect, going back the way you came can be a pretty successful strategy once you realize you've lost your way. This is true whether you're lost in the woods or a city or a mall or a park. (It's not so good at sea. You can't really say, "Well, then we turned left at that one wave. Remember?") The problem with backtracking is that it takes patience and constant awareness of your surroundings—and those are often the first two things that fly right out the window when someone realizes that they're lost. It also doesn't help that many lost people seem disinclined to backtrack, as we've seen. Either they think they don't need to, because their destination is just around the corner (spoiler alert: it isn't), or they don't *want* to, because going back would be an admission of failure or like walking right back to square one of being lost.

If a lot of these tendencies sound like traditionally male behavior, you're not mistaken. The two groups most likely to be the subject of a search and rescue operation are men ages 20 to 25 and 50 to 60, in that order. All you have to do is spend some time drilling down into the National Park

Service's Annual Search and Rescue Dashboard to experience the truth of those numbers.[32] In 2017, for example, there were 319 search and rescue operations just in the state of Utah's national parks. Of those 319, the majority were men, and the majority were in their 20s. Way to go, fellas!

To be fair, though, it can be really hard to find your way out of places like Utah's national parks, what with their changes in elevation and topography and all the intersecting animal and human trails that crisscross their many hundreds of thousands of acres. Even experienced hikers who do everything right can get themselves lost when they come to a juncture where different paths converge and then diverge again. Rabbit path? Donkey path? Human path?

That's what happened to a Tasmanian hiker named Andrew Gaskell in 2016 when he decided to climb Mount Mulu in Malaysia's Gunung Mulu National Park. Gaskell summited the 7,795-foot mountain on the morning of his second day in the park. At the top, he took some pictures, then turned around and headed back. Only a few kilometers from home base, in an area where multiple streams crossed the path that led out of the park, Gaskell says he "took a wrong turn, and despite my efforts to backtrack I couldn't find my way."[33]

Despite his vast experience hiking throughout Tasmania— or perhaps *because* of it—Gaskell proceeded to "wander through the jungle, looking for a way out." He started random

....
[32] You *could* spend all that time digging through their data, or collect some anecdotal data by watching a dad or granddad.

[33] It's not like the wilderness has a "back" button that takes you down the right version of backward.

26

traveling. *For. Days.* And rather than finding his way home
he later said that all he did was lose his bearings even more.

While random traveling is not uncommon after backtracking has failed, what is unusual, at least according to
Dr. Hill's research, is the extent to which Andrew Gaskell
wandered. "Only a few lost persons—such as some school-
age children by themselves—will continue to move ran-
domly during their ordeal,"[34] Hill wrote in the introduction
to his book *Lost Person Behaviour.* "Most lost people show

---

[34] Don't be THAT kid.

somewhat more purposeful behavior in their attempts to get out of the woods."

VIEW ENHANCING

The process of ascending to high ground to get a better look at the surrounding area definitely qualifies as one of Dr. Hill's so-called purposeful behaviors. It's a method for getting your bearings that is favored both by experienced outdoorspeople and movie characters marooned on deserted islands. As a matter of fact, on Tom Hanks's very first day on the South Pacific island in the movie *Castaway*, he climbs up to the island's highest point to get a better look around.[35] Eventually Andrew Gaskell did the same thing. Unfortunately, what both guys discovered was just how lost and alone they were.

When view enhancing didn't work for Gaskell, he did a little direction traveling, moving west with the sun until he ran into the river that marked the western border of the park, at which point he followed it south to the park's entrance. That was the plan, anyway. Unfortunately, he couldn't hold his direction because "the forest canopy made it hard to keep track of the sun [and] the landscape was a frustrating matrix of mountains and rocky streams." So,

....

[35] Of course, the behavior of Tom Hanks's character was being controlled by a writer/god and lives in a universe generated and stored on a hard drive, but it was a writer/god who did their research and we can respect that. And, truth be told, maybe the story's the same for Andrew Gaskell, who knows?

Gaskell continued to wander about for several more days, where others might have used particular points on that matrix of mountains and streams as a base from which to employ two other lost person behaviors: route sampling and direction sampling.

ROUTE SAMPLING

At the convergence of multiple trails or paths or streams, the lost person picks one of the branches and travels down it as far as they can without worrying that they won't be able to find their way back to the place where the trails intersected. If the lost person is carrying a bucket of Day-Glo paint or some other brand of daytime fluorescing paint and a brush suitable for painting on rough surfaces like tree bark, they may consider painting a marker on a tree located near the intersection so they can easily find their way back.[36, 37] This may not be an option for most lost people, however.

If that first path doesn't pan out or run into anything familiar, the lost person returns to their base of operations,

....

[36] When painting a mark on a tree to serve as a marker for base camp, paint a one-foot square patch on the tree, using two coats to ensure maximum coverage. Allow the first coat to fully dry before applying the second coat. If the mark is not quite square or is out of plumb, scrape the bark off the tree where the mark has been painted and move to another tree to try again. Continue this process until a well-formed square has been painted or there are no more trees in the area. In the latter case, the lost person may consider random traveling once more until they come to another intersection with plenty of trees.

[37] Josh is the only person who thought this was funny and he stands by it.

perhaps demarcated by a painted tree, and tries another route. They repeat this process until they've exhausted all the paths or they've found their way out.

DIRECTION SAMPLING

This is the same as route sampling, in that the lost person is traveling out from the same point of origin every time, except it isn't paths or waterways they are following: just cardinal directions. Typically, someone engaged in direction sampling tries never to go so far that they lose sight of whatever landmark they chose to start out from.[38] That's very limiting when trying to navigate through a forest or a Bornean jungle. That's why people who try direction sampling often get re-lost and end up random traveling again for a while, until they finally pick a new landmark and try direction sampling again. Persistence is the key to staying lost.

If you're anything like us, this list of lost person behaviors probably makes a lot of sense, while at the same time inspiring zero confidence that if someone gets lost, no matter how much they know, they will ever be able to find their way home on their own. That's why the eighth and final survival strategy for when you're lost is the one recommended most strongly by safety programs and park rangers and search and rescue personnel: For the love of God, just stay where you are.

....

[38] A tree, for instance.

STAYING PUT

If you haven't deliberately slipped off the grid, like Christopher McCandless when he walked into the Alaskan wilderness in the spring of 1992, there should be a decent expectation that a search party will be organized once your friends and family and the relevant authorities agree that you have officially been gone way too long. If that is true, by far the best thing you can do once you realize you're lost is to stay right where you are and sit tight, because if there is anything more difficult than finding a needle in a haystack, it's finding a needle that keeps moving around.

And yet, staying put is almost always the last thing people do. It goes against nearly every instinct we have. *Not* doing something is not something we humans can easily do. We have to move. We have to act—unless you're super lazy, which could benefit you here. Even experienced outdoorspeople, who know that hunkering down is the best strategy when they're disoriented, admit that they probably wouldn't stay put as a strategy. Andrew Gaskell certainly didn't. He spent his entire thirteen-day ordeal lost in Mulu National Park wandering, climbing, probing. Not once did Gaskell really consider simply sitting down and waiting for the Malaysian SAR team to arrive. In the event a person is found sitting in one place, it's rarely because they were being cautious and humble, or because they actually thought it was a good idea. It's usually because they are exhausted or injured or asleep or pouting.

As part of the research for his book, Dr. Hill studied more than 800 missing person reports from the Nova Scotia area where he teaches. In those 800 reports, he found only two instances where the lost person purposely stayed put in order to be found. One was an 80-year-old woman who got lost almost immediately upon entering the woods; the other was an 11-year-old boy who had received Hug-A-Tree training[39] at school.

Wanna guess how old Andrew Gaskell was when he got lost in Malaysia in 2016? He was 25. Typical male.

Okay, that's all. Now go get lost in another chapter!

....

[39] Hug-A-Tree was created in the early '80s by an empathetic US border agent and search and rescue expert after the 1981 death of nine-year-old Jimmy Beveridge, who got lost in the woods during a camping trip with his family and died of hypothermia. If hugging a tree seems stupid, get over it. A life-saving tree deserves a hug.

CHAPTER 3

~~~~~~~~~~~~~~~~~~~~~~~~~~~~~~~~~~~~

DEMOLITION DERBIES

WHY WE LOVE TO WATCH THINGS GO BOOM!

A demolition derby is bumper cars for grown-ups by way of the Thunderdome—many cars enter, one car leaves. Long before the X Games or extreme sports or Mountain Dew X-Treme or Mountain Dew MDX,[40] even before monster truck rallies came along, demolition derbies were serving up literally explosive spectacles to anyone who enjoyed watching large machines crash into each other at high speeds.

Which, face it, is most of us, since inside even every ostensibly mature adult is a small child who just wants to watch things go boom.[41]

....

[40] Mountain Dew X-Treme was an extremely dark purple grape-flavored version first sold in Kuwait in 2010 before spreading to other parts of the Middle East like an extreme wildfire of taste. Its slogan was "Do You Dare?" Mountain Dew MDX was a short-lived energy drink that contained an extreme amount of caffeine.

[41] Search your feelings. You know it to be true.

It was this particular insight that stock car driver Larry Mendelsohn says he had when he supposedly invented the demolition derby in 1958 at New York's Islip Speedway. Larry noticed that many race fans paid more attention to the crashes than the actual races. So why not, he thought to himself, make up a sport to fill the time between races where the car crashes were the whole point? As Larry later put it when talking about the race cars, "People absolutely love to see them crash. Whenever there's an accident on a corner you have a crowd gather around.[42] You can imagine what the crowd would be like if there were 100 cars, all in one night, deliberately crashing against one another." But Larry is underselling his own genius. It's not just 100 cars crashing into each other. It's 100 cars crashing into each other over and over and over again!

It's a great story, but there's a good reason to believe Larry wasn't actually the first to come up with the idea of smashing automobiles into each other. That reason is called facts.

WHERE WE'RE GOING, WE DON'T NEED ROADS

No one seems to know who actually staged the first demolition derby. Some say it was a celebrity motor sports promoter named Don Basile, who put on a derby full of famous racers

---

[42] This reminds us of that famous Weegee photo of the crowd jostling for a better look at a dead body that we talked about in our "Crime Scene Photography" episode.

at Gardena's Carrell Speedway in Southern California in 1946. Others believe it was used car dealer (and owner of a magnificent nickname) "Crazy Jim" Groh from Franklin, Wisconsin, back in 1950.[43] Whoever it was, by 1953 the concept was common enough that the term "demolition derby" made it into the Merriam-Webster dictionary—which kind of makes Larry Mendelsohn's claim to a 1958 invention as shaky as a ten-year-old full of Mountain Dew MDX.

It's easy to see how the idea might have developed when you consider that a very similar kind of proto–demolition derby, called a "crash derby," had been going on at county fairs across America since the thick of the Great Depression in the 1930s—which is not an era when you'd expect to see people wrecking still-usable cars for fun. Still, everybody needs a distraction when times are tough, and crash derbies were a cheap form of entertainment that satisfied a long-standing thirst[44] among American spectators for what one sociologist called "reenacting technological destruction for public amusement." Or what we called, approximately four paragraphs ago, people's desire to watch things go boom.

These crash derbies did not just suddenly appear whole out of the ether, either. They were expansions of what you might call crash jousts—two cars driving head-on into each

---

[43] We're considering adopting our own nicknames, "Crazy Josh" Clark and "Crazy Charles W. 'Chuck'" Bryant. Write in to let us know if you endorse the idea or if you feel it's insensitive.

[44] Just like Mountain Dew can satisfy your long-standing thirst. Honest, this chapter isn't sponsored by Mountain Dew—or is it?

other, or "a terrible idea." Crash jousts had become popular in the early 1920s thanks to a handful of daredevils who performed stunt-driving exhibitions at local racetracks and fairgrounds for slack-jawed locals to enjoy. Groups with killer names like Ward Beam's Daredevils, Lucky Lott's Hell Drivers, and Jimmie Lynch Death Dodgers would jump buses, drive through walls of flame, roll cars on their sides, and then drive into each other at full speed. It was good-paying work if you could get it.

STUFF YOU SHOULD KNOW . . .

This is the text of an ad placed in a New York–area newspaper in 1931:

WANTED: Single man, not over 25 years, to drive automobile in head-on collision with another car at the Albion Fairgrounds in connection with the Congress of Daredevils on August 19. Must crash with another car at 40 mph and give unconditional release in case of injury or death. Name your lowest price. Write B. Ward Beam, Albion, N.Y.

If you can barely imagine what seeing two old-timey cars crashing head-on into one another at 40 mph would be like, prepare for further amazement! Crash jousts too had an antecedent. Between 1896 and 1932, a number of people decided that staging train wrecks—prearranged crashes between locomotives—was a good idea. Organizers would lay track nearly a mile long, then engineers would start locomotives facing each other at either end of the track and jump to safety before they crashed into each other. Spectators would pay to watch the devastation and

then scramble to collect a souvenir from the wreckage after the demolished locomotives came to rest, hopefully not on fire.

At one staged locomotive collision in Ohio, 25,000 people showed up.

At another outside Waco, Texas, organized by the brilliantly named William Crush, 40,000 people were lining the track when the locomotives' boilers exploded on impact like massive hand grenades, sending hot metal shrapnel more than a thousand feet through the air at tens of thousands of feet per second, and killing two people. An eyewitness who also happened to be a Civil War veteran was quoted as saying it was "more terrifying than the Battle of Gettysburg," which, as you may know from our episode on the Gettysburg Address, was the bloodiest battle of the entire war.

Train collisions crawled, so crash derbies could walk, so demolition derbies could run.[45] And while they clearly existed in one form or another before Larry Mendelsohn's event in Islip, it is true that they really took off after he began staging them on a regular basis. By the 1960s, ABC was airing the Demolition Derby World Championships on its popular *Wide World of Sports* program. In the '70s, the Los Angeles Coliseum hosted a demolition derby on national TV, organized by none other than Don Basile. Much as he had for his 1946 derby, Basile recruited famous racers for this one too.

Indy 500 racing champions like A. J. Foyt, Mario Andretti, Parnelli Jones, and Bobby and Al Unser participated—but unlike his first derby, or any derby really, where drivers competed in cheap, beat-up old cars, the champions in Brasile's derby drove expensive vehicles, including a Rolls-Royce donated by the famous daredevil Evel Knievel.

In 1975, derbies started gamin' it up with the release of an arcade game called *Destruction Derby*. Even the icon of 1970s cool Fonzie, from the popular TV show *Happy Days*, got in on the trend when he fell in love with professional derby driver Pinky Tuscadero. When the Fonz gives your

---

[45] So video games could soar. *Destruction Derby*, *Wreckfest*, *Grand Theft Auto Arena War*, even *Mario Kart* gets in on the smash, bash, and crash destruction.

fake sport two thumbs up and a full-throated "aayyyy," you know you've hit the big-time.[46]

Derbies began to wane in popularity in the 1980s, as commercial real estate development led to the demolition of many of the old tracks where derbies took place. But they made a comeback in the 1990s as a popular event at state and county fairs, returning to their roots, so to speak. They eventually peaked at around 5,000 derbies a year in the US, with between 60,000 and 75,000 demolition drivers competing annually for prize money ranging from a few hundred bucks to tens of thousands of dollars.

ORDERING THE CHAOS

Whenever there are trophies and money to be won, there must also be rules. Lotteries and sweepstakes are highly regulated, for instance. The Laws of the Game for international football (you know, soccer) are more than 220 pages long. Baseball has eleven rules just about the uniforms. Demolition derbies are no different, though fittingly for something so chaotic, the rules tend to vary widely.[47] Still, most derbies share a number of key guidelines, some

------

[46] The exception to this rule is stunt water-ski shark jumping. In a season five episode, the Fonz (actually his stunt man) jumped a shark on skis and jump-started an idiom that now means the moment when a show (or something) starts to lose popularity—usually because they did some desperate stunt to try to keep folks hooked.

[47] We found the rules sheet for the demolition derby that was held at the 2009 Harrison County Fair in Iowa and it had thirty-six different stipulations for car preparation.

of which raise serious questions about the kind of person who needs these rules spelled out in the first place:

DRIVERS MUST BE AT LEAST SIXTEEN YEARS OLD.

DRIVERS MUST WEAR SEAT BELTS.

DRIVERS MUST WEAR HELMETS;
FOOTBALL HELMETS DO NOT COUNT.

NO HEAD-ON CRASHES.

NO INTENTIONAL HITS TO THE DRIVER-SIDE DOOR.

DRIVERS MUST CRASH AT LEAST ONCE EVERY
TWO MINUTES.

ALL GLASS MUST BE REMOVED FROM VEHICLES.

ALL CARS MUST HAVE WORKING BRAKES.

NO DRIVER CAN PARTICIPATE DRUNK.

Once the drivers and their cars meet those oh-so-rigorous standards, everyone typically lines up around the edges of a dirt arena or track, which has usually been soaked with water to keep the dust from flying, while the crowd chants a countdown. Most drivers will start with their front end facing away from the center of the arena, with the intention of spending as much of the derby as possible in reverse, smashing into the other cars with their rear bumper.[48] It's

----

[48] Demolition derbies are, as you may have already concluded, no place for an old Ford Pinto (with or without flaming death bolts), a Chevy Sonic (no matter what a daredevil hedgehog has to say about it), or a Mercedes-Benz smart car (not smart!).

not that this is a better strategy for inflicting more damage; it's a life-extension strategy designed to spare the radiator, carburetor, and engine from repeated collisions. Once those go, your day is done.[49]

When the green flag drops, drivers begin crashing into each other at speeds up to 30 miles per hour. That doesn't seem like a lot when you consider the average speed of a NASCAR crash or a highway pileup, but a collision even at that low speed can produce 8,500 pounds of force, which would be like getting slammed in the chest by a good-sized adult male hippopotamus.

That same crash will also simultaneously produce 30 to 40 G's of pressure in the 30 milliseconds of deceleration after impact.[50] In physics, this is called "no fun." And yet the expectation is that everyone signed up for a demolition derby will crash as often as they need to in order to disarm their competition and take the checkered flag. Failure to do so means being disqualified. Avoiding as much contact as possible as a strategy for winning is called "sand-bagging" and it is scorned by honest demolition derby fans. With rules like these in place, and a stiff dose of social pressure from the fans, a typical derby takes around 20

---

[49] Any usable parts that remain will be harvested from the car, and the driver is likewise harvested for their organs.

[50] One G equals the acceleration of gravity. To give you an idea of what 30 G's might feel like, roller coasters typically produce only 5 G's on their steepest drops, so this amount is far, far harder on the body and can produce blackouts. There's a cool calculator online that lets you plug in your basic pre-crash stats so you can scare the crap out of your parents! https://www.omnicalculator.com/physics/car-crash-force

minutes to complete. In the Thunderdome-iness of it all, the last car still running is declared the winner.

THE INFAMOUS INDESTRUCTIBLE IMPERIAL

Many derbies, especially the bigger multiday ones at county and state fairs, will have multiple events that feature different categories of car and racer: There are women's, RV, fire department versus police department, compact car, and truck events. But the most common derbies involve those full-sized cars from the 1960s and 1970s that are sometimes referred to as land yachts. They aren't their own event classification per se, it's just that the most popular cars in the main event tend to be post-1965 American hardtops, station wagons, and sedans with long front and rear ends that offer extra smashability.

But there is one car from this broader genre that is banned, to this day, from nearly every derby held in America: the Chrysler Imperial. Specifically, the 1964 to 1966 models, but also some of the later models from the 1970s. You may know that we are not car guys, but we can appreciate the Chrysler Imperial. It strikes fear in the hearts of any derby driver unlucky enough to face off against it—especially when they're not behind the wheel of an Imperial themselves—because it is built like a tank. Its body-on-frame construction[51] makes it heavier, sturdier, and more resilient on uneven terrain.

Its V8 engine delivers 500 lb/ft of torque and sends it at the competition like one of those locomotives from the turn of the century.[52] The Imperial's body also sits up a

[51] This means (we looked it up) that the body of the car that contains the passengers is built separately and then mounted to the frame of the vehicle that contains the axles, steering column, etc., rather than built as one whole piece. Thus, the body can move independently of the frame.

[52] Torque (we looked this up too) is the same type of force you apply to a wrench to turn it. That type of force is handy not just for tightening nuts and bolts but also for cars because of the way they produce power. Car engines turn a crankshaft, which spins the same way it would if a wrench were turning it. That then turns the axles, which make the wheels on the bus go round and round, which make the car go vroom. Lots of torque is useful in making a car accelerate quickly and it is the power that gets heavy cars like the Imperial to move at all.

little higher because it's mounted onto the frame instead of having the frame incorporated into it, so when it's hit from behind, the impact drives its bumper upward, which pushes its wheels down into the ground, giving it more traction. The Imperial is like Invincible Mario but with power, mass, and that time-honored ability to make things go boom. It's almost like it was designed for demolition derbies.

The interesting thing about the ban on Imperials in demolition derbies is that it has nothing to do with increasing the risk of injury to the other drivers. No, it's strictly about their unstoppability. In fact, derby officials say that serious injuries and deaths are rare—a 2004 study found that drivers sustain fewer neck injuries than you might expect (though you might expect that all of them have neck injuries,[53] so anything less than that feels like a win). A lower-than-expected incidence of neck injuries doesn't change the fact that cars can flip over and burst into flames, however, putting drivers at risk of just a few other injuries, including sizzled skin and organs.

If you're not deterred by the slight possibility of accidentally dying in a car that you crash on purpose, well then, there are plenty of derbies still being staged all across the United

....
[53] Their parents probably think they need their heads examined at the very least.

States and around the world for you to enter.[54] Of course, there is that pesky "at least sixteen years old" rule. It's far safer than taking part in an organized train collision, that's for sure. Assuming you can even find one nowadays, what with parents being so overprotective and the government not letting you own your own train.[55]

....

[54] Before entering any demolition derby, we must insist that you fill out our Demolition Derby Indemnity Waiver at the back of the book, which frees us from any legal liability that may arise should any misfortune befall you from entering a demolition derby after reading this chapter. If your copy of *Stuff Kids Should Know: The Mind-Blowing Histories of (Almost) Everything* does not include the Demolition Derby Indemnity Waiver, please send in for a replacement form. Write to Consumer Information Catalog, Pueblo, Colorado 81009.

[55] Fewer than 100 people in the US own their own private railcar, and none of them owns a complete locomotive.

~~~~~~~~~~~~~~~~~~~~~~~~~~~~~~~~~~~~~~

CHAPTER 4

FACIAL HAIR

THE LONG AND SHORT OF IT

There are really only two types of facial hair: beards and mustaches. Every style of facial hair you've ever seen is one of these two, or a combination of both.

Think about it like part of a scientific classification of human traits that we just made up but totally makes sense. Here, facial hair is a family, beards and mustaches are each a genus, and their many varieties are individual species that could interbreed, as it were, to create hybrid subspecies like the duck-billed platypus of the facial hair family, the soul patch.

This might seem self-evident when you take a second to think about it, but then why would you be thinking about this at all unless you work in the relatively booming beard care industry or you're a pogonophile—a lover of beards and the bearded. The *Economist* wrote about that very philia in a 2015 article about the growing trend of beardedness while reporting from the National Beard and

Mustache Championships, which were taking place that year in Brooklyn . . . obviously.[56]

The beards the *Economist* reported on were part of more than just a passing trend. Facial hair grew more popular over the rest of the decade until it became a full-blown phenomenon of twenty-first-century maleness. It even had a cameo in the coronavirus pandemic that started to spread around the globe in early 2020. Media outlets stumbled on a 2017 infographic from our friends at the Centers for Disease Control right here in our hometown of Atlanta. The infographic showed which facial hair styles were okay with a standard face mask and which styles were less ideal because they "crossed the seal," allowing all manner of nasty little things access to your wide-open mouth.[57]

Infographics are neat, especially the unintentionally interesting ones, and this particular one got our attention. It shows thirty-six distinct styles:

Fourteen mustaches, twelve beards, nine beard-mustache hybrids, and a clean-shaven option. When we noticed that more than two thirds of these styles were less than optimal for proper mask usage, the chart revealed something we hadn't thought of before: Facial hair doesn't seem particularly functional, at least not in the way we typically think about functionality in the high-tech, go-go,

....

[56] A year earlier, in February 2014, the *New York Post* ran a story about men in Brooklyn paying as much as $8,500 for facial hair transplants in order to grow better beards.

[57] Sleep tight, don't let the beard bugs bite.

47

N95-mask-wearing world of today.[58] And if that's true, then the question is: Why do we have facial hair at all?

It's here that we found, to our great excitement, that scientists aren't exactly sure. But they have come up with a best guess that makes a lot of evolutionary sense, if you take a step back to see the forest for the trees—or the beard for the whiskers, as it were.

PUTTING THE "FUN" IN FUNCTIONAL

As it turns out, facial hair is not a functional physical human trait in the way we thought it was for many years. It's an ornamental one. In fact, of all the physical features on the human body—including other kinds of hair—facial hair is the only one that is purely or primarily ornamental. That is, it doesn't actually do anything or perform any kind of specific physiological function. Just take a look at what the rest of our hair does for us:

- **Body hair helps with thermoregulation (it keeps things cozy).**
- **Head hair protects your scalp from the beating sun, but also traps heat in if you're in a cold-weather climate.[59]**
- **Eyelashes are like screen doors for the eyes, keeping bugs and dust and little debris particles out.**
- **Eyebrows stop sweat from getting in your eyes.**

....

[58] Our sincere hope is that this reference becomes dated and future readers are entirely confused by it.

[59] This is particularly true of helmet hair.

- **Armpit hair collects and disseminates pheromones (think of those as perfume made by the body) while acting like the WD-40 of body hair, reducing friction between skin on the underside of the arm and skin on the side of the chest as we walk and swing our arms.[60]**

- **Pubic hair also helps reduce friction, as well as provide a layer of protection from bacteria and other pathogens who try to tunnel their way into private parts.**

But facial hair? You will notice it doesn't appear on that handy list of adaptive hairy traits.

In the early days of studying this kind of stuff, evolutionary biologists thought it might serve thermoregulatory or preventive purposes similar to body hair and pubic hair.[61] Beards and mustaches are around the mouth, after all, and the mouth takes in food and other particles that might carry disease. Beards and mustaches are also on the face, which is connected to the head, which loses a lot of heat out of its top if it isn't covered by hair. It all makes sense when you look at it that way.

Except there's a problem with this theory: It leaves out 50 percent of the population, i.e., females. Natural selection

....

[60] Learning this has made us feel bad about the bare underarm beauty ideal that women in the West have traditionally been expected to follow.

[61] Beard and mustache wearers do get some of these benefits, but they are secondary and incidental to their primary purpose. For instance, clean-shaven men are three times more likely to carry the nasty bacteria called MRSA on their faces, but it's not because beards protect you better from the bacteria. It's that shaving scrapes the skin and leaves small open wounds that are much better at collecting pathogens. [Josh shudders.]

is ruthless, and it has sent A LOT of species the way of the dodo—for instance, the dodo[62]—but rarely, if ever, does it select for a trait in a species and leave half the population hanging, especially the half that brings new life into the world (i.e., the more important half). If facial hair were meant to perform important functions, it would be present across both sexes. Instead, thick, mature facial hair is present almost exclusively on the male half of the species, and its only job is to sit there on the face of its wearer as a signal to everyone who crosses his path.

WHAT'S THE FREQUENCY, KENNETH?

What signal does facial hair send? Well, here's where it gets a little complicated, as ornamental traits go. University of New Mexico professor Geoffrey Miller, one of the preeminent evolutionary psychologists in the field, put it this way: "The two main explanations for male facial hair are intersexual attraction (attracting females) and intrasexual competition (intimidating rival males)." Basically, facial hair signals one thing to potential partners (namely health, maturity, and ability to make babies, hubba hubba–type stuff) and something else to potential rivals (formidability

....

[62] Nature is an extinction machine, something to think about next Earth Day. We want to save the big blue marble, but it doesn't care one way or the other if we slide right off. In fact, more than 99 percent of all species that have ever lived in the entire history of Earth (about 5 billion of them) have gone extinct.

and wisdom or godliness[63]). Taken together, these signals elevate the status of the men with the most majestic mustaches or the biggest, burliest beards.[64]

The signal that facial hair sends also tends to be stronger and more reliable between males, who are more commonly rivals, than it is between males and females, who are more commonly partners. In fact, evolutionary biologists will tell you (if you ask them) that while some females really like facial hair, and some don't, and some couldn't care less, more often than not, attraction has as much to do with beard density as anything else. That is, if you're in a place where there are a lot of beards—say, a lumberjack convention—then a clean-shaven face is more appealing, but if you're surrounded by bare faces, then a beard is best.[65]

Scientists who study how traits change over time noticed that when a trait is rare within a population and it sticks around, it tends to gain an advantage. In guppies, for example, males with a unique combination of colored spots mate more often and are preyed upon less. Double bonus! What a huge competitive advantage.

The downside is that very quickly there are tons of baby guppies with that cute color combo of spots—which means the trait loses its rarity. Not to worry, nature has

....

[63] Maybe this is why we always depict God with a beard? Something else to think about next Earth Day.

[64] Just ask Chuck, he'll tell you!

[65] This is one of the big reasons men who are special forces operators have developed such outsized reputations—they get to sport facial hair amid a sea of regular soldiers who must be clean-shaven at all times.

a solution for that: As more guppies bear that same trait, fewer gal guppies think it is oh-so-cute and more predators recognize that colored spots signal supper. In other words, what was once the hot new guppy thing becomes old news.

This yo-yoing back and forth between common and uncommon explains why the attractiveness of facial hair varies so much from population to population. It also explains why understanding intersexual completion helps us understand the purpose of facial hair. It's not enough simply to be attractive: You also have to be more attractive than the people around you, and in enough of the right ways to stand out.

This goes a long way toward understanding the ebb and flow in the popularity of facial hair across time. Sporting a killer 'stache or a bushy beard is only effective, evolutionarily, as long as it still makes you part of the hot new guppy thing around the pond. When it makes you old news, it's time to put the razor to work.

HEY, MAN, I (DON'T) LIKE YOUR STYLE

Throughout history, people have donned facial hair or shaved it as a response to the choices of their enemies and rivals. The ancient Romans went clean-shaven for 400 years because the ancient Greeks, their rivals during the Hellenistic period, celebrated beards as symbols of elevated status and high-mindedness.[66] For the 270 years the English lived under threat of Viking invasion (and, in some parts, actually lived under Viking rule), a period from 793 to 1066 CE tellingly called "The Viking Age of Invasion," Englishmen went clean-shaven as a cultural reaction to their bearded Viking invaders. During the Protestant Reformation, many Protestants grew out their beards in protest against Catholicism, whose priests were typically clean-shaven.

What's even more fascinating is how great an impact rulers and other high-status individuals have had on facial hair trends. The emperor Hadrian brought beards back to Rome in the second century CE and the entire leadership class of the Roman Empire followed suit, including a number of Hadrian's successors. In the Middle Ages, Henry V was the first king of England to go clean-shaven, and because he was such a great monarch, English society and the subsequent seven kings followed in his beardless footsteps. It wasn't until Henry VIII came along, in all his egotistical, extravagant, murderous glory (we need to do an episode on him), that the beard made a comeback, undoubtedly as a way for him to distinguish himself from his predecessors.

---

[66] Interestingly, it was Greece's own warrior-king, Alexander the Great, who seems to have kicked off this beardless trend. Legend has it that Alexander and his men shaved prior to the final battle against the Persians for control of Asia because he realized the enemy could grab them by their beards during close-quarters fighting. The reality is that Alexander shaved because he was trying to fashion himself after the young, beardless Heracles (Hercules, to the Romans) from mythology, and he wanted his men to draw strength and inspiration from his embodiment of demigodliness. No ego there.

It's not just facial hair, yea or nay, where the choices of rulers and other high-status people have affected the choices of those around them and for generations to come. You can see it in the evolution of specific facial hairstyles as well. Remember that chart of facial hairstyles issued by the CDC in 2017? Each style has a name. Nine of them—a full 25 percent—are named after influential figures, mostly in the arts. A few of the styles have normal names, but are so obviously connected to the one or two prominent people who made them famous that you're more likely to identify the popularizer than you are the "official" name.

STUFF YOU SHOULD KNOW . . .

ABOUT POLITICAL PHILOSOPHY

The Great Man theory of history, advanced by a nineteenth-century Scottish philosopher named Thomas Carlyle, held that leaders and rulers have an outsized impact on the direction of the story of humanity. Others say it just seems that way because those are the people whose deeds are more likely to be recorded—history is written by the victors, after all—and as such, they are the ones who are still reported on centuries later. In the realm of facial hair, however, it really does seem to be the case that leaders and rulers had an outsized impact on trends, since they were frequently the social influencers of their day. And what's more social than a nice beard/mustache combination?

DALI

Dali, twentieth-century Spanish surrealist painter known for his melting clocks and insanely long formal name, Salvador Domingo Felipe Jacinto Dalí i Domènech.

ZORRO

Zorro, fictional early twentieth-century masked man who sported a Cordovan hat, a sword, and a cape for good measure. Zorro is the Spanish Lone Ranger; that, or the Lone Ranger is the American Zorro. Either way, the Lone Ranger didn't have any facial hair.

WALRUS

Popular in the late nineteenth century, thanks to men like Mark Twain and Teddy Roosevelt; when modern-day observers see the Walrus, their first thought is of Sam Elliott or the Lorax.

ZAPPA

Frank Zappa, 1960s counterculture musician known for his involvement in the freak scene and for having four kids with super-cool names (Moon Unit, who recorded the hit song "Valley Girls," which we discussed in the "Vocal Fry" episode, Dweezil, Ahmet Emuukha, and Diva Muffin).

VAN DYKE

Anthony van Dyck, eighteenth-century Flemish painter known primarily for portraiture.

CHEVRON

They call it the Chevron, but really, they should just call it the Magnum P.I. and get it over with, because Tom Selleck is the man who almost singlehandedly made mustaches popular again in the 1980s.

BALBO

Italo Balbo, marshal of the Italian air force under Mussolini. Bet you didn't know that one.

GARIBALDI

Giuseppe Garibaldi, nineteenth-century Italian folk hero best known for his role in the unification of Italy.

VERDI

Giuseppe Verdi, nineteenth-century Italian composer best known for his operas *La Traviata* and *Aida*. Giuseppes are well-represented in this list, turns out.

BANDHOLZ

Eric Bandholz, twenty-first-century beard-related entrepreneur and founder of an online magazine called *Urban Beardsman*. You can also call this one "the Chuckers."

TOOTHBRUSH

The Toothbrush, that's what we're calling this? Really? Maybe some of the credit should go to a certain short, charismatic comedian from the 1930s. Charlie Chaplin was one of the biggest stars of silent films—ever!

CHIN CURTAIN

It is a travesty that the Chin Curtain is not called the C. Everett Koop.

HOW TO START OR END A FACIAL HAIR TREND

Changing tastes and the influence of high-status men in competitive environments are all well and good, but nothing moves the needle one way or another on the popularity of facial hair like a good crisis. Indeed, it was the coronavirus pandemic that brought the amazing CDC chart to our attention, and not in the most positive way. London's *Daily Mail* published a piece about it under the headline "Could your facial hair put you at risk for coronavirus?"[67] This is not the first time facial hair has fallen under scrutiny in the midst of a disease outbreak. In a 1916 piece in *McClure's* magazine,

---

[67] Pro tip: Anytime you see a news headline that ends with a question mark, the answer is almost always NO.

one doctor managed to blame facial hair for the spread of nearly every communicable disease known to humanity. "There is no way of computing the number of bacteria and noxious germs that may lurk in the Amazonian jungles of a well-whiskered face," he said, "but their number must be legion." With more column inches, who knows what other ailments the good doctor would have tied to beards. Reporting like this tends to generate a rising tide of clean-shaven faces.

Then sometimes, a crisis goes the other way and leads to a period of increasing beardedness: a period like the one that produced the 2015 *Economist* article about pogonophilia, the CDC facial hair chart in 2017, and the expansion of the National Beard and Mustache Championships in 2019 from eighteen categories to forty-seven. The crisis that created this increased facial hair growth? The 2008 global financial crisis.

As banks failed, facial hair grew. As savings accounts got smaller, beards got bigger. Why is that? Well, those same evolutionary psychologists who will tell you about the attractiveness of facial hair will also tell you that there is no more important time to signal your fitness to rivals and potential partners than during times of crisis.[68]

So what happens to facial hair when a health crisis meets a political or an economic crisis? Your guess is as good as ours, but if and when it happens, you can be pretty sure it's going to look funny.

....

[68] Makes you wonder what was going on in the guppy world when those colored spots became the hot new thing.

exact.[69] The Paul McCartney the world had been hearing with his Beatles bandmates on the radio and seeing on magazine covers, on television shows, and in concerts since then was actually a lookalike. The remaining Beatles had brought him in to hide Paul's tragic death—though, conveniently, not without leaving a bunch of clues about the insane cover-up hidden within the lyrics of their songs and the artwork of their album covers, including *Abbey Road*, which had come out a month earlier.[70]

This late-night caller had "proof" too. Proof is in quotes on purpose, by the way, for reasons that will make sense by the end of this paragraph. He told the DJ, Russ Gibb of WKNR-FM, that if he put on the White Album and played the "Number 9" intro at the beginning of "Revolution 9" backward, he would hear John Lennon saying "Turn me on, dead man."

"Proof!"

....

[69] Interestingly, this was the day that John Lennon met his future wife, Yoko Ono. So, if you're one of those miserably unhappy Yoko haters out there who thinks Yoko Ono broke up the Beatles, you'd probably say that something died on November 9, 1966.

[70] If you don't know who Paul McCartney is but this story still sounds vaguely familiar, no worries—you're thinking of Avril Lavigne, another singer who supposedly disappeared and was secretly replaced back in 2003.

~~~~~~~~~~~~~~~~~~~~~~~~~~~~~~~~~

CHAPTER 5

BACK-MASKING

WHEN RECORDING BACKWARD IS MOVING FORWARD

Late on October 12, 1969, a man called into a Detroit radio station and blew the lid off a story that had been making the rounds on American college campuses for more than two years.

Paul McCartney was dead.

Paul McCartney. *The* Paul McCartney. The singer, bass player, and songwriter for the Beatles. You know—John, Paul, George, and Ringo—the guys who sang those smooth old songs like "Hey Jude," "Let It Be," and "Yesterday."

Paul was "the cute Beatle," and in March of '69, he broke about a jazillion young hearts when he married a lady named Linda Eastman.

But this story claimed that Paul had died in a car accident nearly three years earlier. November 9, 1966, to be

1969: ANOTHER CRAZY YEAR FOR THE BEATLES AND FOR MANKIND

JANUARY	The Beatles perform together for the last time, on the roof of Apple Records.
MARCH	• James Earl Ray admits to killing Martin Luther King Jr. • Sirhan Sirhan admits to killing Robert F. Kennedy. • John Lennon and Yoko Ono get married.
JULY	• Apollo 11 lands on the moon. • Ted Kennedy lands in the waters off Chappaquiddick Island, tragically killing Mary Jo Kopechne.
AUGUST	• The Manson Family murders a bunch of celebrities. • The Troubles begin in Northern Ireland. • Woodstock happens.
SEPTEMBER	• John Lennon quits the Beatles. • The *Abbey Road* album is released.

OCTOBER	• The Zodiac Killer murders his last confirmed victim. • The Amazin' Mets win the World Series as one of the biggest underdogs in sports history.
NOVEMBER	Paul McCartney gives an interview to *Life* magazine addressing the "Paul is dead" rumors and mentioning for the first time that the Beatles had broken up.
DECEMBER	• The Vietnam War draft lottery begins. • Final members of the Manson Family are apprehended.

Gibb did as the caller urged, heard what the caller suggested, and fell down the rabbit hole that would come to be known as the "Paul is dead" conspiracy.[71] The story of Paul's death dominated Beatles-related news for the rest of 1969. It got so crazy that at one point John Lennon called into WKNR to debunk the story and Paul had to come out of

---

[71] Gibb was no mere one-trick pony. In addition to launching the "Paul is dead" phenomenon, he ran the Grande Ballroom, the psychedelic rock music venue in Detroit in the '60s. He also helped launch the career of bands like MC5 who basically are the reason we have punk rock. Well-rounded guy.

seclusion in Scotland, where he was holed up with his wife, Linda, and their newborn daughter, Mary, to confirm that he was, indeed, still alive.

Since then, looking into the clues of the "Paul is dead" conspiracy has become a rite of passage for every new generation of Beatles fan. Its lasting nature, we think, is because what ultimately propelled the conspiracy into the mainstream were those backward messages. As creepy as they are, though, it's something that actually finds its way into music fairly often. It even has a name: backmasking.

Backmasking is a practice that involves recording any kind of sound—vocals, an instrument, a sound effect—then taking that snippet of audio, flipping it around, and placing it wherever the artist wants within a given track. The definition is the encoding of materials on a recording in a way that it can only be understood properly when the recording is played backward.[72] In practice, it's not that it's more easily understood this way; it's that sometimes—most of the time—it just sounds cool.

TURN LE BEAT AROUND

The technique of backmasking has its roots in a form of musical composition called *musique concrète*, pioneered in the late 1940s by a composer in the French national radio system named Pierre Schaeffer. This form of music was made

---

[72] We talked a lot about backmasking and the like in our excellent—if we do say so ourselves—episode, "Was the PMRC censorship in disguise?"

possible by the increasing availability and versatility of tape recorders after World War II. Tape recorders captured sounds on a strip of tape that was magnetic. The beauty was that if you screwed up, you could rewind and rerecord over your oops.

The idea behind musique concrète was that you recorded any kind of natural sounds[73] that you found interesting—hitting two blocks together, banging a copper pot, flicking one of those springy rubber-tipped door stopper thingies that make your cat go bonkers. Then you could manipulate and splice those sounds together by cutting and reassembling the tape until you had an arrangement that sounded good and maybe even sounded like music.[74]

Musique concrète techniques were soon adopted by avant-garde musicians in the 1950s and eventually spread to a handful of popular musicians in the 1960s. Would you like to guess who two of those popular musicians were? We'll give you a hint: They're named after apostles and they formed the Beatles. John Lennon and Paul McCartney were so intrigued by the pioneers in this kind of music that they put a picture of one of them—a German composer named Karlheinz Stockhausen—on the cover of the *Sgt. Pepper's Lonely Hearts Club Band* album.

See, the guy who called into WKNR that night in October 1969 wasn't totally nuts after all. The Beatles actually did

----

[73] This is sometimes called "found sound," as in sounds found naturally . . . in nature.

[74] Many consider musique concrète to be the Big Bang of electronic music.

experiment with backmasking, and some of it did make it into their albums. What's funny is that it got there, at least in the beginning, entirely by chance.

It started during the recording sessions for the *Revolver* album in the spring of 1966. First, when they were laying down the track "Rain," John came home late one night, and put the tape of that day's recordings on backward on his reel-to-reel player. He liked the sound so much that he played it for the band the next morning—and they liked it so much that they backmasked lyrics onto the fadeout of the song.[75] A month later, a similar thing happened while recording "I'm Only Sleeping," when the tape operator mistakenly put a tape into the machine backward. Everyone loved it and George Harrison worked into the night rewriting his guitar part so they could flip it on the track and get the sound they were looking for.

Revolver became the Beatles' most experimental album. On nearly every song, you can hear some kind of recording or production trick, many of them with their roots in musique concrète.[76]

THE ORIGINAL TROLL

This is when backmasking starts to come into its own. Two years after *Revolver*, the Beatles released the White Album, which contains the track "Revolution 9," which fans are

[75] The technical term for this part of a song is "coda."

[76] "Rain" and "I'm Only Sleeping" became the first pop tracks ever to have backmasked lyrics and guitar, respectively.

convinced has the phrase "Turn me on dead man" back-masked onto the beginning. Here's the thing about that:

"Revolution 9" is full of found sounds composed by Lennon and McCartney in the style of musique concrète, which—if you'll remember from, say, a page or so ago—is where backmasking gets its start. And the song does in fact have backmasking in it. It's all backmasking, really, using all those found sounds, just not any of the kind that the conspiratorially minded among us might be thinking of. Is it any wonder, then, why the "Paul is dead" rumors never really went away? They were built on something that actually existed and that the Beatles were actually doing at the time.

For the next thirty years, many artists would follow the Beatles' lead and experiment with backmasking. Dozens, however, would be accused of far worse than using backmasking techniques to hide the accidental death of a bandmate. Like inserting satanic lyrics into their songs, for instance.

Artists like Led Zeppelin, Queen, the Eagles, Pink Floyd, Deep Purple, ELO, Cheap Trick, Slayer, Judas Priest, Black Sabbath, Motörhead, and our favorite, Styx, all used backmasking, to the delight of teenage boys around the world. A few of these certainly contained some dark messages, while others were much lighter in their tone.

Regardless of the actual message, things got so bad by the mid-1980s, thanks to pressure from religious organizations and parents' groups like the Parents Music Resource Center (PMRC), that congressional hearings were held, lawsuits were filed, and the recording artists at the center of it all got super PO'd.

There is an old saying: Never argue with someone who buys ink by the barrel. There should probably be a corollary to that: Never get into a shouting match with someone whose job involves a microphone. Because that's what they're going to use to fight back. In this instance, all the hip bands of the day got even with their accusers by doing exactly the thing they were accused of. Motörhead, Iron Maiden, and Frank Zappa each subsequently planted backmasked lyrics aimed directly at groups like the Parents Music Resource Center[77] as a show of defiance. The Beatles backmasked the line "Turned out nice again" into their recording of "Free as a Bird" in 1995 on the fifteenth anniversary of John Lennon's murder just to troll them.

"We even put one of those spoof backwards recordings on the end of the single for a laugh," Paul said, "to give all those Beatles nuts something to do."

The champ of trolling misguided groups like the PMRC was the English rock band ELO. After being accused of planting messages on their 1974 album *Eldorado*, they dropped two on their next album, including the phrase "The music is reversible, but time ... is not. Turn back! Turn back! Turn back! Turn back!" Following that, in 1983, they released an entire concept album full of backward and hidden messages with the rather obvious title *Secret Messages*.

....

[77] The PMRC drove the Senate hearings in 1985 that delved into obscenity and parental advisory. Seriously, check out our episode "Was the PMRC censorship in disguise?" You. Will. Love. It.

I DON'T THINK THAT MEANS WHAT YOU THINK IT MEANS

When you read stories about the "Paul is dead" controversy and the backmasking claims at the center of it, one of the things you will run into time and again is a description of Beatles fan behavior as an example of a passionate fan base simply getting carried away in their zeal.[78] There's definitely something to that explanation, but there's also something deeper going on. In psychology, it's called *pareidolia*, or the tendency to see or hear things in totally random objects or sounds.

On the visual side of things, this phenomenon is at the heart of the Rorschach inkblot test and is responsible for

....
[78] Also, these fans were known to use drugs.

our tendency to see shapes in clouds. It's why people so frequently see Jesus or the Virgin Mary in all manner of objects.[79] Though, weirdly, it's in food where the Lord pops up most often: Since 1977, the list includes a flour tortilla, a grilled cheese sandwich, a Cheeto, and a pierogi.[80]

On the auditory side, pareidolia explains our willingness to believe that a Siberian husky with his own Instagram page can say "I love you." Or why two different commenters on a hearing loss discussion forum described hearing voices in their air conditioning units. And it's why, in 2008, Fisher-Price pulled its talking "Little Mommy Real Baby Cuddle & Coo" doll from the shelves when a parent heard it speak the words "Islam is the light." Of course, each of these people was

---

[79] Probably the most famous of these is the Shroud of Turin (a piece of linen with a faint image of a man on it and believed to be the cloth Jesus was buried in).

[80] If you believe Jesus died for your sins, it makes sense that he keeps showing up in carbs.

mistaken, just like Russ Gibb was mistaken when he insisted he heard what his late-night caller told him he would hear on those supposedly backmasked White Album tracks.

The question, though, is why did any of them hear anything at all? Most experts believe it's because our brains are geared to try to make sense out of randomness, to find order in the chaos. The unknown is scary: We like to feel that there is intention and meaning to the things we don't understand. It makes us feel safe.

Carl Sagan postulated that our tendency to see faces everywhere—and, by extension, to hear voices in every sound—is a survival mechanism. You can certainly see the evolutionary logic in that theory. In the wild—or Florida, same difference—survival very much depends on a person's ability to identify friend or foe as quickly as possible, with as many senses as possible. Pareidolia is recognition that our brains have this bias hardwired for at least two senses—sight and sound. In other words, it makes much more sense to see the face of a potential enemy hiding in the bushes than it does to under notice such things and let your enemy get the drop on you.[81]

All of which we get. What we don't understand is why, when we see something in the randomness, it's always God, but when we hear something in the randomness, it's always the Devil. Not sure there is a name for that phenomenon, backward or forward, but it's definitely real.

....

[81] We know this sounds pretty paranoid, but blame nature, not us.

CHAPTER 6

~~~~~~

AGING

DO WE GOTTA?

They say there are only two certainties in life: death and taxes. Judging by the laws and scientific innovations of the twenty-first century, however, there seems to be a third certainty: that people will do everything humanly possible to skip both.

Especially the death one, though that's not surprising. We've always known that people will hang on to this mortal coil by the very tips of their fingernails with everything they've got.

It's a basic survival instinct, one that probably emerged somewhere early in the 3.5 billion years of the evolution of life and soaked into every living thing on Earth, humans included. But as G.I. Joe would say, that's only half the battle.[82]

What good is living for a long time if you're going to be sick for a whole big chunk of it at the end? Who wants that? Nobody. And that's really what we're talking about when

....
[82] Chuck would like to point out that the 12-inch G.I. Joe doll remains superior to the 3.75-inch G.I. Joe action figure. Josh disagrees, yet they remain friends.

we talk about aging. It's not just about extending lifespan, it's about increasing healthspan—and how expanding healthspan elongates lifespan.[83]

LIFESPAN **VERSUS** HEALTHSPAN

The first-known use of the word *lifespan* appeared in 1831. At the time, the average global life expectancy was a mere 29 years (40 if you were lucky enough to be born in the United Kingdom—think about why that mattered). In order to raise the average life expectancy beyond what we consider young adulthood today, humans waged an extraordinary battle against death in the twentieth century. Through a combination of advancements in medical care,[84] hygiene,[85] food production,[86] and social welfare policy,[87] life expectancy around the globe jumped from 32 to 66 years between 1900 and 2000.[88] In the US, it went from 49 to 76 years. Japan was the true success story, though. Despite the devastation of completely

---

[83] It's okay if you need to read this sentence a few times. It took us a few attempts to write it.

[84] Thank you, Elizabeth Blackwell.

[85] Thank you, John Snow.

[86] Thank you, Upton Sinclair.

[87] Thank you, Frances Perkins.

[88] This was quite an accomplishment considering the first half of the century featured two of the deadliest wars in human history—both of which were fought principally by men in their twenties, which definitely drove down the average lifespan in those years.

bombed cities, capped off by two atomic bombs, the country ended the century with the highest average life expectancy in the known world—81 years. When she passed away in 1997 at age 122, France's Jeanne Calment—a smoker!—had held the title for the world's oldest person for four years.[89] More than 25 years later, Calment's record remains intact. And imagine if she never smoked!

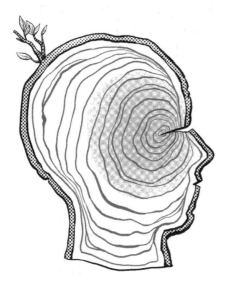

For some scientists, as they evaluate all the advances that have been made since her death and the fact that her record still stands, Jeanne Calment's extraordinary age has seemingly set the outer limits of a human lifespan.[90]

---

[89] In 2018, Calment's claim was challenged by a Russian glassblower named Nikolay Zak. He claimed that Calment was a fraud and was in fact Jeanne's daughter, Yvonne, who had supposedly died in 1934 at age 36. Under Zak's theory, it was really Jeanne who had died in 1934, and Yvonne assumed her mother's identity to avoid paying an estate tax on her inheritance, carrying on this masquerade among friends and family for 60 years. The French strenuously dispute this claim and Calment continues to hold her record.

[90] Technically, it was set back in 1825 by a numbers nerd from England named Benjamin Gompertz, who noted that the risk of death increased exponentially with age, doubling every eight years and reaching 50 percent by age 101. If you follow this to its conclusion, there comes a point where it is impossible to survive—well, at least according to the statistics.

MYSTERIOUS MATH

A common fallacy when it comes to interpreting statistics is that the word "average" means "typical." It doesn't. Average life expectancy means the average age of death among the entire population, taking into account the age of every person who died that year.

For example, if you have ten people and six of them died at age 2 and the other four died at age 50, the average age of death of that group would be 21.2 years. But no one died at 21 (or anywhere near it)! To solve this math trick, you take the number of deaths in an age group and multiply it by that group's age of death (e.g., 6 x 2 = 12 and 4 x 50 = 200). These products are added together (12 + 200 = 212) and divided by the total number of deaths (212 / 10 = 21.2).

Usually when you see a low average life expectancy, it means many children died at birth or in childhood. Their deaths greatly outnumbered the people who survived to an old age, and that pulled the average lifespan down, down, down.

DECADE	MALE LIFE EXPECTANCY	FEMALE LIFE EXPECTANCY
1900s	47.9	51.1
1910s	49.4	53.7
1920s	57.0	59.5
1930s	59.8	63.4
1940s	63.7	67.9
1950s	66.3	72.3
1960s	66.8	73.7
1970s	68.5	76.2
1980s	71.0	78.1
1990s	72.8	79.1
2000s	75.0	80.2
2010s	76.3	81.2

Not everyone has bought into that idea, though, which brings us to healthspan.

The first-known sighting of the term *healthspan*—defined as the length of time that a person is healthy—is at the beginning of this chapter. Not really, it was in 1931. This was two years deep into the Great Depression, when few people were thinking about healthy living and most people were just focused on surviving. Not surprisingly, the term didn't get much use for most of the twentieth century because after the Great Depression came the second great war (WWII), and after that came a period of insane abundance with new things like microwave dinners,[91] fast food,[92] remote controls,[93] and smoking on airplanes—all meant to remind us that we'd beaten Nazism and to trick us into thinking we were invincible. People weren't thinking about health, and they certainly weren't thinking about healthspans. They were just happy to be alive, let alone living longer.

It wasn't until the end of the century that "healthspan" started making quiet appearances alongside its more famous companion. Still, it had to wait around until the first Baby Boomers (remember those kids who grew up with Mr. Potato Head?) started hitting 65 in 2011 before anyone really took notice of it. Boomers, the first generation to hang out at health clubs[94] and visit cosmetic surgeons for face-lifts, started asking why they should stick around longer if all it meant was a slow death by disease? They didn't just want to see their grandkids twice a year and putz about until the grim reaper knocked, maybe winning a few bingo games along the way if they were lucky; they wanted to keep their

....

[91] Thank you, Percy Spencer.

[92] Thank you, Walter Anderson and Billy Ingram.

[93] Thank you, Nikola Tesla.

[94] We are purposely not including the wealthy folks and their earlier health resorts (see our live episode "The Kellogg Brothers' Wacky World of Health"), because they were just making up what health and wellness meant as they went along.

party going.[95] So they made 70 the new 50 and waged war against aging.

By the time "healthspan" finally made its Webster's dictionary debut in 2018, 10,000 Americans were turning 65 each day. People were paying close to $200 billion for antiaging treatments. And, a Harvard geneticist named David Sinclair had figured out how to reverse aging in mice (more on that later, we promise). The quest to live both longer and healthier had become the #1 objective in rich countries. Fortunately for those obsessed with it, it was also becoming a serious scientific endeavor that was showing real possibilities.

TWO STEPS FORWARD, FOUR YEARS BACK

One of the great advances in the twentieth century was a pretty much continuous upward climb in life expectancy, which is why it was particularly alarming when, from 2014 to 2017, life expectancy actually went down for three straight years. The last time that had happened in America was the four years around World War I. What made this grim statistic more alarming was that the US wasn't involved in any major ground wars to speak of during this period—certainly nothing like WWI. And, don't forget, 2014 to 2017 was also in the middle of an era where healthspan was exploding across the Western world.

....
[95] They were the generation that started out as hippies, then moved on to disco.

Researchers found this decline in American life expectancy came from a depressing mix: There was an increase in eight of the top ten causes of death—things like heart disease, stroke, diabetes, and the flu—along with the rise of the opioid crisis and an increase in suicide. Opioids (drugs prescribed for pain relief) are extremely addictive. By this point, the number of deaths by opioid overdose had more than quadrupled since 1999, and all deaths attributed to opioids were up by a factor of six (!). Suicides were up by a third.

THE AGING QUESTION

But let's back up for a second. To understand how to extend a healthy lifespan, you first have to understand its natural rival, aging. What exactly is aging? What makes us become all the things we can't imagine: old, wrinkled, weak, out of fashion, committed to getting up at the butt crack of dawn?[96] And why the heck do old folks age anyway?

For many of us, it's aging's long-standing association with

---

[96] It turns out there is an answer to why grandparents get up before the garbageman. Aging people produce less melatonin, a hormone that helps us go to sleep and stay asleep. A decrease in melatonin, along with an increase in pain, nocturia (having to get up in the night to pee), and all sorts of other unpleasant extras conspire to rob the aged of their sleep. All of which reinforces why research into how to expand healthspan is a legit public good.

time, which is itself inescapable, that gives us the impression that aging is inevitable. Except, there's more to it than just the simple passage of time.

Even though it has the word *age* in it, aging isn't really about the number of trips we've taken around the sun. On our birthday, people don't say we aged a year—they say we're a year older. Similarly, when we see someone for the first time in years and they look great, we say "you haven't aged a bit." That's because aging is really about the change to our physical condition—on the outside and on the inside—over time.

If you read several dozen scientific articles on aging, you'll see they all agree, aging is a decline in function that 1) is based on time and 2) continues till death—a real bummer from start to finish. Experts consider aging to be a cause for a whole assortment of chronic diseases such as cancer, diabetes, and heart disease. The thing is, they do not consider aging itself to be a disease. That little nuance, it turns out, is the frontline of a very robust and ongoing debate about the nature of aging—whether we can stop it or even possibly reverse it,[97] and whether we have to do it at all.

....

[97] Is it worth it? Let science work it out and we'll see.

DAUGHTER CELLS

Let's get nosy and peek in on what it takes to make a daughter. We're not talking about the birds and the bees stuff—count on your folks to tell you about that—we're talking about daughter cells. To do that, we need to peer into the nucleus. You know, the control center of the cell where the genetic information is stored.

Genes are the stretches of DNA that code for all the characteristics that make you, you. Like your hair color, eye color, and, apparently, how you age. Inside the nucleus DNA is bundled up in bunches called chromosomes.

To keep a body healthy, cells have to copy their DNA, then divide into two daughter cells. Take your skin, for example. An adult body loses 200,000,000 skin cells a day. To replace those, it takes a lot of copying. Copy. Copy. Copy. But just like with copying a list of spelling words, there's a chance of mistakes. A chance the DNA gets damaged.

Whatever their position in this debate, pretty much everyone in the scientific community refers to a 2013 article from the journal *Cell* that identified three categories that characterize aging: primary hallmarks, antagonistic hallmarks, and integrative hallmarks.

There are primary hallmarks—the things that cause damage in cells and in genes. One of the primary hallmarks is telomere attrition.[98]

Telomeres are like those plastic tips on the end of your shoelaces,[99] but for chromosomes. They are at the tips of the chromosome and help make sure the DNA gets copied properly. Telomere attrition is when they start to wear out and shorten. Just like your shoelaces are pretty much toast when those plastic tips wear out, the same goes for cells and telomeres—because as telomeres wear down, your cells stop dividing and your tissue stops regenerating.

There are antagonistic hallmarks—the ways our bodies respond when damaged. One peppy example is deregulated nutrient sensing. What a mouthful! That's a less-than-artful way of describing when the body forgets to be good at taking in nutrients. This is usually because the system for storing excess energy goes on the fritz. Say your brain sends out signals that make you crave food when your body doesn't need it. It keeps sending the signal until it gets what it thinks you need—but by then obesity has set in, and diabetes will follow shortly thereafter. Antagonistic!

And then there are integrative hallmarks—what happens when all that damage from the primary hallmarks and all those icky effects from the antagonistic hallmarks start combining and become too much for the body to manage.

....

[98] Great name for a rock band. Well, so-so, at least.

[99] These plastic tips are called "aglets" and they date back to Roman times, though an English inventor from the 1790s named Harvey Kennedy often gets the credit for them.

That's when exhaustion starts to happen, and the cells responsible for healing injuries just kind of run out of gas.

When you add all of these hallmarks up, you get aging; pretty much everyone agrees on that. What they disagree on is what we can do about it.

HELLO, DOLLY

Some researchers—let's call them Team Cumulative DNA Damage (CDD)—argue that aging is genetically programmed. Their view is that the adding up of damaged DNA that happens as telomeres shorten and cells get less good at dividing results in aging, which results in death. Team CDD's ultimate proposition is that aging is essentially irreversible because our genome has suffered permanent wear and tear. The best we can do is slow down the aging process (and elongate healthspan) through exercise and diet. Team CDD dominated the second half of the twentieth century. Then, in 1996, Dolly the Sheep was born—well, cloned.

Dolly was supposed to show off all the possibilities of the future, human cloning, body part harvesting, and all that stuff you see in the movies. Instead, her big contribution was debunking long-held beliefs.[100] You see, before Dolly, new animals had only ever been grown from cells from an embryo. An embryo is an early stage of development, so young it doesn't yet have all of its major body parts.

....
[100] This is not to say that Dolly conducted any studies or wrote any papers herself; rather, she contributed simply by existing.

Since she was grown from a regular old cell, Dolly's birth and life proved that just about any given adult cell had all the DNA necessary to give rise to another animal. Which meant that you could reprogram an adult cell to act like an embryo cell. Which meant the idea that DNA damage was irreversible was bunk. Which meant Team CDD's theory was—oh, okay, you get it.

Although Dolly didn't bring about the dark world many predicted,[101] she did set the stage for a second set of researchers—let's call them Team Information Loss (IL)— that would become a formidable opponent to Team CDD. Team IL scientists argue that even if Dolly hadn't man-aged to fully discredit the DNA Damage theory of aging, Team CDD's theory still misses the mark—because the epi-genome, not the genome, is the central player in aging.

....
[101] . . . at least, not yet . . .

A cell's DNA is made of three billion pairs of letters. How's a cell supposed to know which parts to read? Special chemicals tag different parts to be read. Those chemicals, called the epigenome,[102] act like bossy parents, telling cells exactly what to read and, thus, what they will become. When a cell loses that guidance, which happens when we age, the genes that are supposed to be turned off turn on and vice versa. Chaos ensues. Chronic diseases appear. Dogs and cats living together. Death comes ripping.[103]

Team IL argues that we humans can defeat aging once and for all if we can learn to reset and reprogram our epigenome. It makes sense: Problems with epigenomes create a whole avalanche of issues that trigger all of those hallmarks of aging that the *Cell* study identified. So if we can stop those problems with epigenomes from ever beginning, we can forestall the avalanche and, hence, the hallmarks of aging. And won't the old folks be happy then!

When news of Dolly the Sheep's birth made headlines, Japanese biologist Shinya Yamanaka got to work developing a biological cocktail that could reprogram a cell's epigenome back to its original form. Yamanaka first used the technique on mice. Astoundingly, a year later, he was able to successfully reset human skin cells to infancy.

....

[102] Epigenetics is the basis for one of our better (and better titled) early episodes, "Can your grandfather's diet shorten your life?"

[103] If you didn't recognize this as a reference to a Misfits song, it's time for you to listen to more Misfits.

BIOLOGICAL AGING AND CHRONOLOGICAL AGING

Thanks to discoveries like Yamanaka's cocktail, we now each have two ages, believe it or not. One is the age we celebrate with cake and ice cream—the number of trips we've taken around the sun by our birthday. The other is the age that an epigenetic clock says we are, based on our health.

In 2011, a UCLA researcher named Steve Horvath stumbled on a way to measure aging. Essentially, Horvath was able to take a sample of DNA, measure just how many chemical tags had been added, and run the results through the computer, maybe go get a cup of coffee while the machine did its thing, and then—presto!—arrive at an estimated biological age. For the first time we were able to see the true impact of the epigenome on the aging process. If your epigenetic clock (from in your cells) said you were older than your chronological clock (from the calendar), you were aging faster than you should and probably needed to make some changes. If it said you were younger, you better watch out or else your younger brother or sister will soon be "older" than you!

Once Horvath's Clock, as it came to be known, was able to show our biological age, the stage was almost set to begin testing whether that clock could be stopped or reset. Almost.

Yamanaka Factors and Horvath's Clock are both now

and forever named after their originators[104] — and both were important in the antiaging breakthrough that Harvard geneticist David Sinclair later made (it took us a while, but we're back to him, just like we promised).

Think of an old cell like a cell phone with scratches crisscrossing the screen. There's still info in the phone, you just can't read it (or play any of the games, bummer). Unlike a trashed screen, Sinclair thought there must be a repair job for aging cells.

To test his theory, Sinclair got his hands on a pair of young mice and "scratched" the epigenome of just one of them. He did not bother the other one. In a matter of a month, the mouse with the scratched epigenome began to show all the aging signs of a middle-aged mouse. Within two or three months, the mouse looked downright sick. By the end of a year, its hair was grizzly gray, it developed wrinkly skin, diabetes, memory loss, dissolving bones, and it probably even started waking up at 4:45 a.m. too, the poor thing. When Sinclair checked the wrinkly mouse's age using Horvath's Clock, he found it was 50 percent older than its sleek, slim, stylin' partner, who was living the good life.

Okay, so Sinclair managed to artificially age a poor mouse — pretty impressive. But the big question was whether he could prevent aging. Apparently, he had the same thought, because he rummaged through his molecular toolbox looking for something that would repair the epigenome.

....
[104] Unlike Horvath, Yamanaka won the 2012 Nobel Prize for his achievement. Poor Horvath.

He came up with nicotinamide mononucleotide (NMN), an almost magical molecule that lets a cell do stuff like turn sugar into energy. Sinclair thought it might just do the trick.

He thought right. After two months of treatment, the aged mouse experienced a 56 to 80 percent bump in endurance for things like running.[105] After being treated with NMN, wrinkly mouse could run as fast as and significantly longer than its untreated partner. When Sinclair and his team ran the DNA through Horvath's Clock, the mouse had effectively de-aged.

The next step was to reverse aging back beyond chronological age. Imagine that mad scientist working in a deep, dark dungeon. With an evil laugh he picked up a mouse by the tail and crushed its optic nerves. (Okay, we doubt his laboratory was in a dungeon and he surely didn't laugh, but for the good of science, he did do that dirty deed to a mouse.)

Then Sinclair shook up a nice batch of Yamanaka's biological cocktail and injected it into the mouse's damaged eye. The results were electrifying. The nerves didn't just wake up—they reset themselves. The mouse could see as well as it could when it was young. In fact, it was young. The clock confirmed as much.[106]

....

[105] Mice haven't been the only ones to benefit from NMN. Even though it hasn't been fully tested, Sinclair has been using it on himself for years, and while we don't yet have the results, the man is 50, looks 40, and is a tender 31 according to the epigenetic clock.

[106] Sinclair has since repeated the de-aging process on practically every part of a mouse's body. You should see the ear!

So where does this leave us? Can we stop aging, and even reverse it?

Will we ever be able to reset our entire cellular system? Between NMN and Yamanaka's cocktail, it certainly feels like we're heading in that direction. As Sinclair put it: "Ultimately there is no upward biological limit, no law that says we must die at a certain age." Which can mean only one thing: 123 years old, here we come. Watch out, Jeanne Calment![107]

[107] If that really is your REAL name!

CHAPTER 7

THE PET ROCK

THE SAVIOR OF 1975 (OR THE DUMBEST TOY OF THE BEST DECADE)

Are you a cat person or a dog person? Do you let your pet run free, or do you pride yourself on all the tricks you can teach them? Do you want a pet that will hunt every squirrel that infiltrates your neighborhood,[108] or one that will play fetch with you for hours? Or do you want a warm fluff-ball to curl up and take naps with?

Maybe you don't fit into any of these categories and would prefer a pet that matches your room (consider a chameleon) or your clothes (how about a leopard); maybe one that tells jokes (get a parrot) or eats your pop quiz-obsessed teacher whole and slowly destroys the evidence (look into very large boa constrictors).

Or maybe you want the kind of pet that requires no care or feeding or exercise whatsoever. A pet that will never

---

[108] Do not let your cats do this. Outdoor cats are responsible for such wholesale slaughter of birds and small mammals every year that scientists consider them an invasive species (they take over where they don't belong). Chuck and Josh say: Keep your cat indoors!

need a pooper scooper or a cleaning, that will never hack up a hairball on your bed, and that won't pass away and force you to think about that whole "rainbow bridge" thing.

Well, thanks to one enterprising visionary, you might be in luck, because there is an option out there just for you.

THE PET ROCK

In the spring of 1975, a freelance copywriter named Gary Dahl was hanging out in the town of Los Gatos ("The Cats" in Spanish) with a couple of advertising buddies, and they got to talking about how much of a pain it can be to have pets. All the attention you need to give them so they don't get destructive,[109] all the feeding and cleaning they require, all the walks they need (even in the rain). And Dahl would know, as one version of the story goes.[110] With two dogs, two cats, two goats, and two chickens, he and his wife, Marguerite, had basically turned their cabin in the Santa Cruz mountains into a very smelly ark (think: Noah and the flood) full of very broken furniture.

Wouldn't it be great if there was a pet with none of those drawbacks? one of the friends pondered aloud.

Yeah, like with my pet rock, I don't have any of those

---

[109] Positive reinforcement only, please.

[110] There are two versions of this origin story—the other one doesn't mention whether Dahl had pets, one way or the other. We have chosen to believe the version with more details, since: 1) it's more fun, and 2) we were trained to choose the more detailed answer on multiple choice tests. It works!

problems, Dahl joked. *No vet bills except once in a while to scrape off the moss.*

Dahl's friends thought his joke was pretty hilarious, so they all must have been dads. Who else would laugh at a completely ridiculous—i.e., "dad"—joke? But Dahl couldn't shake the feeling that the idea of a pet rock, while silly, wasn't entirely stupid. There was an opportunity here.

This was the mid-1970s and the United States had been through a rough ten years—the Vietnam War, assassinations, protests, Watergate, Hasbro nearly ruining Mr. Potato Head, as you might recall from Chapter 1. People were feeling down and were tired of their problems. Dahl thought that people could use an escape, and maybe a laugh.

He started by writing a training manual for future pet rock owners that was modeled quite literally—and hilariously—on dog training manuals. It included a number of commands and tricks that a pet rock would be a natural at mastering, along with others that would be impossible for it to even attempt.

Sit, stay, play dead—the rock was a prodigy; solid. Fetch, come, shake hands—there was little hope. And "roll over," well, the only way that was going to happen was if you trained your rock on the side of a mountain.[111] But the best

---

[111] One of the neat things we've learned along the way is that mountains are where rocks originally come from. As they crumble and then tumble down into rivers, rocks are carried along, broken down over time, and eventually deposited into the ocean as pebbles and sand, where the waves lap them up onto shores to mix with bits of shell and they become beaches. That little tidbit comes from our "We Are Running Out of Sand and That Actually Matters" episode.

were the instructions for attack training, which we're just going to quote in full from the manual because no amount of paraphrasing can match an advertising copywriter hitting their stride:

> A rock is a loyal, devoted pet that can easily be trained to protect you and your family. Woe be to the burglar or prowler who ventures into the home guarded by a **PET ROCK**—or the mugger who attempts to accost a **PET ROCK**'s master.
>
> When the adversary approaches within arm's length and demands all your money, credit cards, and other valuables follow these easy steps: Reach into your pocket or purse as though you were going to comply with the mugger's demands. Extract your **PET ROCK**. Shout the command, ATTACK. And bash the mugger's head in.

As part of the manual, Dahl proclaimed the advantages of a pet rock over other pets—longer lifespan, shorter training period—and played up each rock's lineage, claiming that they hailed from some distinguished rock bloodline like the pyramids of Egypt or the Great Wall of China. In reality, the pet rocks came from the yard of a sand and gravel company on Rosarito Beach in Baja California, Mexico, where Dahl bought them for a penny apiece.

Being an ad man, Dahl also began dreaming up the perfect packaging for his stone-cold genius idea. He envisioned a cardboard box with air holes in the sides (like pet stores at the mall used for selling plain old boring animals[112]) and complete with a nest of excelsior that the rock could rest in for the ride home. With the help of two buddies, both of whom he somehow convinced to invest real money,[113] Dahl managed to get the final product ready for the San Francisco Gift Show in August of that same year.[114]

---

[112] Yes, there used to be pet stores at the mall and it was pretty great to go visit the cute puppies and bunnies until about the time you realized how terrible those stores were for animals. Lots of states and cities realized too and began to ban pet stores from selling dogs and cats.

[113] One of them, a man named George Coakley, invested $10,000, which was pretty big money in 1975. According to the good people at Westegg Inflation Calculator, it's nearly $50,000 in today's money.

[114] The box ended up taking a shape that was oddly similar to a McDonald's Happy Meal container. Don't mistake that pet for a nugget!

A METEORIC RISE (AND THEN FALL)

The Pet Rock was an instant hit. Dahl came away from the gift show in San Francisco, then the one in New York, with thousands of sales. The high-end department store chain Neiman Marcus ordered a thousand Pet Rocks and stacked them prominently in their storefront windows for the holiday shopping season. Bloomingdale's got in on the act, then smaller retailers followed suit. Even though they were going for a ridiculous $3.95 each, or nearly $20 adjusted for inflation,[115] Dahl could barely keep up with demand.

By October, he was selling thousands a day. By Christmas, sales were up to 10,000 daily and well over one million "pets" were sold in total. Dahl was an instant millionaire, and before long a celebrity too. Johnny Carson had him on the *Tonight Show* twice; he was profiled in newspapers and magazines nationwide; there was even a hit song—"I'm in Love with My Pet Rock"[116]—further entrenching the 1970s as the head-scratchingest, most obviously wonderful decade of the century.

Everyone seemed to be happily in on every joke, pet rock included.

Time magazine wrote about the success of pet rocks as part of a December cover story that explored the American

....

[115] Thanks again, Westegg!

[116] Well, if not a hit, a very popular song at least. The song, by Al Bolt, peaked at #85 on the Billboard Country charts.

shopping surge of the time and "trendy Bloomingdale's," commenting that Dahl's creation was "1% product and 99% marketing genius"—a fact that was 100 percent obvious to anyone paying the least bit of attention. One *Time* reader took the gag further in a letter to the editor three days before Christmas, writing in to say that "it saddens me that there are Americans who would buy a Pet Rock from a prestigious store just for one-upmanship. A true pet lover would take in any rock and give it a good home."

And then, just like that, the clock struck midnight on Gary Dahl's ingenious product and the fun was over. The holiday gift-giving season had come to an end, and by early that next year, the pet rock craze had joined it. Dahl tried to keep it going with a bicentennial edition pet rock (sporting an American flag paint job) and ancillary merchandise like T-shirts and shampoo, but demand dropped off so steeply after the 1975 holiday season that he was forced to give away thousands of unsold rocks to charity.

THE 1970S WERE AWESOME, AND HERE'S PROOF

Toys	If the Pet Rock didn't do it for you, there was always the Stretch Armstrong action figure, released by Kenner in 1976, that basically let you draw and quarter a blond guy in a skimpy swimsuit without having to worry about breaking him. And what was inside Mr. Armstrong? The most '70s substance ever: corn syrup.

Cars	You had two choices: land yachts like the Chrysler Imperial LeBaron and the Cadillac Fleetwood Sixty Special—both of which were so big they drove like boats—or a small, bubble-shaped compact car like the AMC Pacer or the Ford Pinto, which blew up if rammed in the rear.[117]
Music	Disco.[118]
Colors	The "trendy" colors for appliances and home furnishings had names like avocado green, burnt orange, harvest gold, and brown. Just brown. Today, those very same colors are the ones doctors say to look for in baby diapers to make sure their systems are working properly.
Fashion	You really had to work for it on the fashion front, from leisure suits and powder-blue tuxedos to bell bottoms, peasant blouses, and big-collar shirts. But nothing said '70s like a pair of corduroy trousers and a shrink-top macramé vest made out of yarn. Would you like to light yourself on fire from the friction of your thighs rubbing together as you walked, or would you rather smell like a wet dog in the rain? There's no correct answer!

[117] We did a live episode called "Back When Ford Pintos Were Flaming Deathtraps" that will tell you everything you could possibly want to know about a car you couldn't possibly ever want to ride in.

[118] Think: big glittery ball, a booming bass, and dances like "the robot" and "the cha-cha."

TV	This was the golden age for film, but on the small screen, TV was starting to come into its own as well, with a number of iconic series that featured fantastic actors, great action, and socially relevant story lines, though not without a vein of racism running through it, wrapped in a shiny coating of persistent sexism. And still, even considering all that, the '70s managed to spit out some great TV: *Wonder Woman*; *Good Times*; *What's Happening!!*; *M*A*S*H*; *Welcome Back, Kotter*; *Sanford and Son*; *The Six Million Dollar Man*.[119]
Hair	Long, straight hair. Long, frizzy disco curls. The long-feathered Farrah Fawcett hair. Huge perfectly coifed Jackson 5 afros. The Dorothy Hamill wedge. The David Cassidy heartthrob shag. Then whatever you call what the rest of the guys were doing. Just so much hair. And that doesn't even count all the facial hair action . . .

[119] He'd be *The Thirty-Five Million Dollar Man* if the show debuted in 2020. You did it again, Westegg!

The line between news and entertainment began to blur, such that news started to get reported not by journalists but by pretty faces and handsome figures with entertaining personalities. This led to the birth of the human-interest story and hoaxes like the Amityville Horror murders being reported as real, true news. It is not an accident that *Anchorman*, a movie meant to poke fun at this decade, is set in 1975, the same year as the Pet Rock.

STUCK BETWEEN A ROCK AND A HARD PASS

Dahl tried his hands at some other gag gifts, all of them pretty great—among them the "Canned Earthquake," which was essentially a can with a windup device in it to make it jump around. None of them took off.

Even without another hit product, Dahl had made enough money in 1975 to retire from freelancing and do other things. He launched his own creative agency, he started giving motivational speeches about how to get rich quick, he wrote *Advertising for Dummies*, and in 2000 he won the

Bulwer-Lytton contest for intentionally bad fiction writing.[120] But it was the purchase and renovation of a saloon (a fun way of saying bar) in San Jose that was Dahl's dream, and fairly soon thereafter his nightmare.

Years later his wife would say that the whole crazy thing "was great fun when it happened"—the pet rock had unquestionably made him rich and famous—but that he'd developed mixed feelings about the whole thing. See, when people found out he owned that saloon, they would "come to him with weird ideas, expecting him to do for them what he had done for himself. And a lot of times they were really, really stupid ideas." It was an onslaught of stupid—everything from packaged bull poop to copycat ideas like "pet sticks."[121] He could only find escape in retirement to Jacksonville, Oregon, and then in death in 2005.

Pet Rocks are still available online. The company ThinkGeek even developed a USB Pet Rock, which is just a plain rock with a USB adapter sticking out of it. It'd be nice to think Dahl would approve, but he was definitely

....

[120] The Bulwer-Lytton contest invites authors to submit the worst opening sentence to a book they can come up with. Dahl won for this sentence: "The heather-encrusted Headlands, veiled in fog as thick as smoke in a crowded pub, hunched precariously over the moors, their rocky elbows slipping off land's end, their bulbous, craggy noses thrust into the thick foam of the North Sea like bearded old men falling asleep in their pints." That's awfully great, don't you think? Or should we say, greatly awful.

[121] Pet rocks we get, but pet sticks? You can't even put googly eyes on them.

frustrated with being known as the guru of zany business ideas. He once said, "If people would just forget I did the Pet Rock, I'd be happy."

It sure is a good thing nobody wrote an entire chapter about him for their book of interesting facts!

CHAPTER 8

DO(UGH)NUTS

THE HISTORY OF AMERICA'S SNACK FOOD

As the "Princess of Pop," Britney Spears sings, "There's only two types of people in the world: the ones that entertain, and the ones that observe." Britney, the best-selling teenage artist of all time, must know a thing or two about entertaining, but what about the first half of that statement?

Could it be that for all the shades of gray in the world, when it comes right down to it, the important stuff is one or the other, black or white? You see it in games—PlayStation versus Xbox—you see it in phones—iPhone versus Android—you see it in oldies music—Beatles versus Elvis—and you see it in . . . doughnuts?! Or is it donuts?

See there, it starts right out of the gate with this, what is perhaps the greatest tasty sweet treat. From the spelling to how they're made to the variety of flavors to the best brand, do(ugh)nuts[122] are a study in duality.

Dough has been fried in oil and sprinkled with sweet, sugary goodness by countless cultures since at least the

....

[122] We haven't trademarked this spelling yet, but we're considering it.

time of ancient Greece and ancient Rome, if not even earlier by prehistoric Native American societies.[123] But the
first appearance of the term *doughnut* doesn't occur until
the turn of the nineteenth century—and it appears as
doughnut, not *donut*—in the appendix of an 1803 English
cookbook that featured American recipes. It then appears
in a satirical novel by Washington Irving in 1809, called *A
History of New York*, in which his description of early life
under Dutch control includes the description of "balls of
sweetened dough, fried in hog's fat, called doughnuts or
olykoeks."[124]

Most early doughnuts were just strips or balls of dough,
but in the mid-nineteenth century, a New England teen-
ager named Hanson Gregory came up with the idea of
putting holes in the middle of them while he was out on
a ship. His mother, Elizabeth, had been in the habit of
making doughnuts with lemon rind and warm spices like
cinnamon and nutmeg that she would liberate from her
son's ship's cargo. She would put hazelnuts and walnuts
in the center, where the dough was least likely to cook
all the way through—making them very literal "dough
nuts"—and give them to her son and his crew for their
long stretches at sea. Eventually, Hanson one-upped his
mother's culinary inventiveness and started punching

....

[123] It may be the reason humans exist.

[124] *Olykoeks* is Dutch for "oily cakes." It was they of the tulip and the
windmill who brought the food over to New York back when the city
was still called New Amsterdam. (Why'd they change it? We can't say.
People just liked it better that way.)

holes in the center of the doughnuts with the round top of a pepper tin, creating their now-traditional ring shape for the first time.

What inspired Hanson to do this? Was he just bored? Some say he was being frugal with ingredients, which honestly doesn't make much sense. Others say getting rid of the undercooked center made them easier to eat and digest. Maybe he didn't like nuts? Then there is the legend that one day he stabbed a doughnut onto the spoked handle of his ship's wheel, either because he needed both hands to control the ship during a storm or he wanted his snack easily accessible while standing at the bridge. Being a sailor, the ability to tell tall tales is as important as reading nautical charts, so it's likely that both versions of that story are questionable.[125] Nonetheless!

In 1947, on the 100th anniversary of his "discovery," Hanson's hometown of Rockport, Maine, put up a plaque honoring him as the man who "first invented the hole in the donut."

Notice the spelling. "Donut" originally began appearing in the late 1800s as a contraction of the longer, traditional spelling,[126] and became more widespread in the 1920s, especially with bakeries—presumably because three extra letters can take up a lot of space on small storefront windows. "Donut" would pick up real steam only a few years after Captain Gregory's confectionary contribution was memorialized, with the founding of Dunkin' Donuts in 1950[127] by a 34-year-old Boston man named William Rosenberg.

Rosenberg had built a sizable mobile catering business after World War II to serve local factory workers and had come to realize that the bulk of his sales came from two items: doughnuts and coffee. So he opened a shop, originally called "Open Kettle," that was dedicated to selling those two wonderful things.[128] Rosenberg eventually renamed it and the

....

[125] That first ship's wheel story seems particularly suspect, since there's probably never been a human in history who didn't just shove the entire doughnut in their mouth when they suddenly needed the use of both hands. It's like our seventh sense.

[126] Ha ha, "do'nut."

[127] Dunkin' Donuts is actually a contraction of two words (Dunking and Doughnuts). It would contract again, this time from two words to one, when the company shamefully shed "Donuts" from their name in 2018, to simply become Dunkin'.

[128] Could have ended up as Op'n K'ttl'.

business became a quick success. Over the next few decades, Dunkin' Donuts would expand rapidly across the Eastern Seaboard, and the spelling of "donuts" along with it.

Mostly, though, "donut" is a great example of the American preference for simplifying the spelling of commonly used words. It's a long-standing cause that has been taken up throughout American history by luminaries like Benjamin Franklin, Noah Webster (of Merriam-Webster), Melvil Dewey (of the Dewey decimal system), Teddy Roosevelt (of the presidents), and the robber baron Andrew Carnegie (of the Mind-Bogglingly Wealthy).[129] Carnegie went so far as to cofound and fund the Simplified Spelling Board in 1906, which counted among its earliest membership ranks people like Dewey, Mark Twain, and the publisher Henry Holt.[130, 131]

Still, "doughnut" remains the preferred spelling. It's used in print nearly two-to-one, even in American publications. Why that is the case isn't entirely clear, since most dictionaries allow for "donut" as an acceptable alternative spelling. It's possible that many people view "donut" as more of a trademark name, with a capital *D*, à la Dunkin' Donuts, though your guess is as good as ours. As the great William Safire put it in one of his classic *New York Times*

....

[129] Robber barons became filthy rich by stomping out competition, creating greedy monopolies, and ruthlessly using workers. Ironically, many in the nineteenth century also gave away hundreds of millions of dollars. Start listing universities, libraries, museums, and other buildings named after Carnegie to get a sense of his gift-giving habits.

[130] Hey, shout out to our publisher!

[131] It makes you wonder if they were all seeking revenge for failing spelling tests.

"On Language" columns: "Those of us among the elderly . . . spell the circular pastries doughnuts because they are made of dough, not do."[132]

THE SYSK VOCABULARY TEST	
SIMPLE & AMERICAN	TRADITIONAL & FANCY
donut	doughnut
omelet	omelette
plow	plough
program	programme
check	cheque
draft	draught
yogurt	yoghurt
airplane	aeroplane
color	colour
flavor	flavour
favorite	favourite
ton	tonne

[132] Bear in mind that William Safire was all hoity-toity about grammar. A satirical headline once read: "William Safire orders two Whoppers Junior."

aluminum	aluminium
ass	arse
oriented	orientated
q	queue

YEAST VERSUS CAKE

Doughnuts are indeed made of dough and not do, though different doughnuts have different doughs that do different things, about that we do not doubt. The main difference is between yeast doughnuts and cake doughnuts. Yeasties, as no one else has ever called them ever, use yeast to make the dough rise, whereas cake doughnuts use chemicals like baking powder and baking soda.

As a result, yeast doughnuts are light and pillowy. They are typically bigger than cake doughnuts and have a smoother, satiny surface,[133] which allows them to take glazing and chocolate coating much better. The honeycomb structure of their insides—created by air bubbles from the proofing yeast—also makes them ideal for filling. If you're eating a jelly- or a cream-filled doughnut, you are eating a yeast doughnut. Of course, the ultimate yeast doughnut is the Original Glazed made by Krispy Kreme (more below).

Cake doughnuts, on the other hand, are denser—dare

---

[133] How badly do you want a do(ugh)nut right now?

we say, cakier—and better for dunking in your coffee. This dunking method was immortalized by the 1934 romantic comedy *It Happened One Night*, when a journalist taught the high-society object of his affection how to dunk her doughnut just like working-class folk.[134] The biggest advantages with cake doughnuts are twofold. First, they can come in a variety of flavors, running through the doughnut itself in wondrous veins of precious gems of taste—like cherry and blueberry and, oh! apple cider.[135] Second, once the dough is combined and formed, it's ready for the fryer. Yeast doughnuts really only come in one flavor (yeast?) and need time to proof before they get dropped into the oil.

All the earliest doughnuts and doughnut ancestors were yeast doughnuts, for the simple reason that baking with yeast goes back 5,000 years and baking powder wasn't developed until the 1840s—well after the Dutch came over with their oily cakes and unwittingly began the American doughnut revolution. It was baking powder that turned the revolution into an evolution, however, accelerating the doughnut's ascent to the summit of American snack food. There is nothing more American, after all, than being able to make a lot of something faster and cheaper, and that's precisely what baking powder did with the cake doughnut.

....

[134] In 1941, the famous manners expert Emily Post called dunking your doughnut "as bad an example of table manners as can be found." She and William Safire were probably secretly married.

[135] The do(ugh)nut is calling your name, right?

TASTE OF HOME

The ease with which doughnuts could now be made increased their popularity over the course of the nineteenth century, but they grew into an American staple during World War I—in France, of all places—when the Salvation Army set up camp wherever American troops were stationed.

The camps were staffed with female volunteers who made cake doughnuts by the bushel and often delivered them directly to the front lines, hot out of the frying oil, in an effort to give soldiers a taste of home.[136] The women came to be known as "Doughnut Lassies" and the campaign they led was such an overwhelming success that other aid organizations like the Red Cross and the Y(!)M(!)C(!)A(!) followed their lead, further imprinting doughnuts on the memories (and midsections) of America's fighting men.[137]

When American troops returned stateside after the war ended, they brought their taste for doughnuts with them. Demand was so high that doughnuts were regularly being served in places like theaters. Things really took off when a Russian refugee named Adolph Levitt turned his problem (couldn't churn out doughnuts fast enough) into an

....

[136] WWI soldiers were nicknamed "doughboys," but the name did not come from doughnuts. Turns out it's unclear where the name originated—possibly from clay they rolled along the trim on their uniforms to keep it white. When it rained, that clay turned into doughy globs.

[137] In World War II, the Doughnut Lassies were replaced by the Doughnut Dollies, though their role was exactly the same. By either name, they were angels on Earth.

invention (the first doughnut machine). He called his machine the "Wonderful Almost Human Automatic Doughnut Machine" (for real) and put the first one in the window of his Harlem bakery. Lickety-split, doughnuts began popping up in bakeries and delis, at festivals and county fairs all over the country. Levitt was even able to wholesale his doughnuts alongside sales of his machine, building a business worth over $25 million in the middle of the Great Depression.[138]

Doughnuts' rise continued through the '30s. In 1934, the same year Clark Gable started dunkin' up a storm on the silver screen, they were named the "Hit Food of the Century of Progress" at the World's Fair in Chicago. Even more monumentally, that year 19-year-old Vernon Rudolph opened the very first Krispy Kreme Doughnut Company store in Nashville, Tennessee, with his uncle Ishmael, who'd purchased a yeast doughnut recipe from a New Orleans chef with the whimsical name of Joe LeBeau. A couple of years later, Rudolph would move to Winston-Salem, North Carolina, and open his own solo Krispy Kreme shop, establishing it as the official founding headquarters of the doughnut business.[139] By the end of the decade, Rudolph would be wholesaling to grocery stores and bakeries all over North Carolina, and within twenty years Krispy Kreme would be a veritable empire, with twenty-nine factories spread across twelve states, setting up the doughnut versus donut battle that Dunkin' Donuts would eventually win.[140]

Today, Krispy Kreme and Dunkin' Donuts have grown to several thousand locations, not just across the United States but around the world—Dunkin' Donuts alone has over 5,000 locations and sells donuts in thirty-seven different countries. In just the United States, over 10 billion donuts

....

[139] A year later, in 1938, the Salvation Army started National Doughnut Day, celebrated on the first Friday of June, in part to help those suffering during the Depression, and in part to honor the Doughnut Lassies on the twentieth anniversary of the end of World War I.

[140] When the world has more doughnuts and more donuts, does anybody really lose?

are made each year, which comes to about thirty donuts per American citizen—more than that if you leave out babies and those who can't eat gluten.[141] With each donut averaging around 300 calories, that's three trillion donut calories a year! Or 1.2 billion days' worth of the recommended daily allowance for calories. It's simple math: America loves doughnuts. We rest our case.

To some, what makes doughnuts absolutely American is the fact that they are deep-fried hunks of dough with little to no nutritional value that get scarfed down by the dozen, which is true. But they're also descended from a long historical lineage that crosses cultural lines and includes not just ancient Romans and Greeks, not just prehistoric Native Americans and colonial Dutch (olykoek), but also ancient Chinese (youtiao), medieval Arab and twelfth-century Jewish societies (sufganiyot), along with German (cruller), French (beignet), Polish (paczki), and Okinawan (andagi) cooks from across the centuries.

Whether you're a doughnut lover or a donut lover, a yeastie or a cakey, a Krispy Kremer for life or you ride or die for the Dunk, doughnuts are one of the few things in life where neither side is wrong and both sides win—a kind of duality that is as unique to doughnuts as doughnuts are to America.

....
[141] A baby eating a do(ugh)nut is a hilarious thought.

CHAPTER 9

~~~~~~~~~~~~~~~~~~~~~~~~~~~~~~~~~~~

THE JERSEY DEVIL

HOO IS THE MONSTER OF THE PINE BARRENS

Boy do we seem to love us some devils. There is the Tasmanian Devil, which is a carnivorous marsupial and aspirational bad boy for a certain subset of T-shirt wearers. There is the Blue Devil, which is a school mascot. There's the Red Devils, the nickname for the Manchester United football[142] club.

There is the Devil Dog, which is the nickname for a US Marine and a snack cake. There is a Dirt Devil, which is a vacuum cleaner brand. There is a dust devil, which is a small, fleeting ground-based whirlwind. And then there is the subject of this chapter, the Jersey Devil, which is a famously mysterious, awful-sounding creature that has been haunting south New Jersey for years.

Poor New Jersey. Few states take as much guff and get as

....
[142] Soccer

bad a rap as the Garden State. The NFL teams the Giants and the Jets both play in New Jersey, but are too ashamed to admit it, insisting that they are New York teams in defiance of basic geography. In movies and TV, it's the home of fictional mobsters like Tony Soprano and nonfictional reality "stars" like the cast of *Jersey Shore*. As everyone outside New Jersey is well aware, the whole place tends to be treated as a punch line, where the joke is on loud girls with bad spray tans and mama's boys with frosted tips who drop the last vowel on a shocking number of deli items—or so the stereotypes go.

Given its largely dubious reputation, it seems fitting that New Jersey is the only state with an official state demon.

THIS BABY'S A REAL LOOKER

Sightings of the Jersey Devil go back hundreds of years, to before New Jersey was a state and before "Jersey Devil" was even the creature's given name.

Originally it was known as the Leeds Devil, named after a woman called Mother Leeds who lived near the Pine Barrens with her alcoholic husband and twelve children. In 1735, she became pregnant with her thirteenth child. Out of sheer frustration with her circumstances—and who can blame the poor woman—competing accounts say she either shouted to the heavens, "Let this one be a devil!", or she asked the

Devil to take the cursed child since everyone knows thirteen is unlucky.[143]

Why Mother Leeds thought that invoking the Devil's name would help anything remains an open question — perhaps she tried the other guy first and got no answer — but a few months later, on a stormy night, she went into labor and gave birth to what seemed like a normal son. Yet within a few minutes, all her cursing came to pass, as the boy transformed into a horrific monster.[144] It grew to a massive size and sprouted horns, claws, and batlike wings. Its body grew hair and feathers, and its eyes glowed bright red. It turned on its poor mother and killed her, then did the same to the rest of the family and the midwives who attended the birth. Quite a handful, that kid.

Fresh out of victims, the monster baby flew up the chimney like some kind of wicked Santa Claus and disappeared into the Pine Barrens, where it has made its home ever since — scaring all manner of people from hunters to cab drivers, military officers to police and firefighters, and park rangers to passersby.[145]

....

[143] Fear of the number thirteen is called triskaidekaphobia. It's the reason 80 percent of the tall buildings in the United States go directly from the 12th to the 14th floor.

[144] In another version of this story, in which Mother Leeds is a witch and the real father is the Devil himself, the baby comes out of the womb as a horrific monster — but after all, what else would you expect?

[145] The Jersey Devil has seen a million faces, and it's rocked them all, or so glam rock star Bon Jovi would say. Did that Jersey boy know he was using a synecdoche? A figure of speech in which one part (face) stands for a whole (person). Wouldn't his language arts teacher be proud?

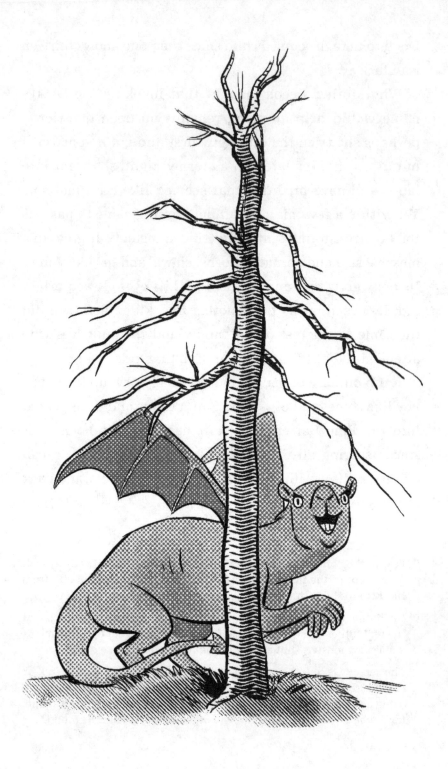

Over time a detailed picture of this heinous beast has emerged from these encounters. Some involved vicious animal attacks, like the one at a pig farm in 1980 where all the pigs had their brains scooped out of the back of their heads as though they'd been attacked by a flying creature with a taste for head cheese.[146] Earlier accounts depicted something resembling a flying goat with wings, horns, a forked tail, a strange hiss, and a terrifying scream that sounded neither human nor animal.[147] A more recent sighting near a New Jersey golf course described a flying llama, who a local caddy said was a big hitter—long—though not much of a tipper.

Perhaps the most famous account of the Jersey Devil comes from Napoleon Bonaparte's older brother, Joseph, who also happened to be the king of Spain for a few years. After losing the Peninsular War to England and being forced to abdicate in 1813, he settled on a lavish estate in Bordentown, New Jersey. While out hunting one day in the Pine Barrens, the elder, lesser Bonaparte noticed strange tracks, like a donkey that walked on two legs, and he decided to follow them, we guess because he wanted to get a load of this walking donkey. It wasn't long before Bonaparte heard a "strange hissing noise" and suddenly found himself face-to-face with a flying creature that had a "long neck, wings,

....

[146] Isn't it crazy how with one simple euphemism we can swip-swap words and politely avoid actually mentioning that it eats brains?

[147] \m/ The sign of the horns, made by holding up just your index finger and pinkie, was popularized by heavy metal bands Black Sabbath and KISS and UT sports fans who were so proud of longhorn cattle.

legs like a crane with horse's hooves at the end, stumpy arms with paws, and a face like a horse or a camel," which hissed at him again before flying away.

WHAT ARE THE PINE BARRENS?

The Pine Barrens earned its name from the sandy, acidic soil in which smaller pine species and hundreds of unique grasses and plants could grow but cultivated crops could not. There are barrens up and down the east coast of the United States as well as some in Kentucky, Wisconsin, West Virginia, parts of Canada, and the Eurasian subcontinent.

All pine barrens lean heavily on fire to clear out undergrowth so that the seedlings of larger, taller species of oak can't take hold and overwhelm the low-growth plant species that need more space and light, both of which get swallowed up by the root system and canopy of large oaks.

Unfortunately for the Atlantic coastal pine barrens—of which the Jersey Devil's habitat is a part—real estate development has cut into the barrens' footprint, and urbanization has led to a general policy of fire suppression

Together, they have made the Pine Barrens nearly endangered. Today it is barely 10 percent the size it was when Mother Leeds's cursed offspring took up residence there.

THE DEVIL'S IN
THE DETAILS

What makes this story even more interesting is that Mother Leeds was a real person. Born Deborah Smith, she emigrated from England near the end of the seventeenth century and married a man named Japhet Leeds, who was the son of Daniel Leeds, a controversial figure in New Jersey politics. Daniel Leeds was a publisher and devout Quaker who came over to America in 1677. A decade after his arrival, Leeds got himself into trouble by publishing a book called *The American Almanack* that included, among other things, references to astrology. Forecasting the future by reading the stars was a definite no-no in that Quaker community. The local leaders suppressed his book. This got Daniel good and mad. He broke with the group and spent the next thirty years or so taunting and satirizing the Quakers in print, making him not only one of New Jersey's first publishers, but also one of America's first producers of "political attack literature."

This earned Daniel a cute little pet name from the Quakers, "Satan's Harbinger," which only made things more difficult for the Leeds family, who were already political pariahs. In addition to publicly demonstrating a fondness for astrology, they'd sided with the widely despised British first royal governor of New Jersey, Lord

Cornbury,[148] which was the colonial equivalent of rooting for the Red Sox while sitting in the Yankee stands.

Then in 1716, Daniel retired and turned the family business over to his youngest son, Titan, who redesigned the masthead of the almanac to include the family crest, which depicts three wyverns—a dragonlike creature with clawed feet and batlike wings—on a shield. See where this is going? Fifteen years later, Titan would find himself in a feud with a young Benjamin Franklin, who was trying to get his own book, *Poor Richard's Almanack*, off the ground by asserting that a series of astrological calculations was predicting that Titan would die in 1733. When that didn't happen, Titan called Franklin out. Franklin claimed that it must be the ghost of Titan Leeds coming after him, since Titan was obviously already dead. So, Franklin.

That year, 1733, happened to be a terrible time to get into a public dispute with Franklin, America's soon-to-be favorite sweetheart, whose voice was beginning to ring out far beyond the streets of Philadelphia as a leader uniting thirteen colonies.[149] It was also the year the British Parliament passed the Molasses Act, which doubled the tax colonists paid for molasses. Molasses was a big deal

....

[148] Cornbury's full name was Edward Hyde, Third Earl of Clarendon. He was widely loathed as a corrupt, immoral thief, accused of "squandering public funds and tax revenues for private purposes" and bribing other politicians.

[149] It must be held against Franklin that he proposed the turkey as America's national bird.

because of one word: rum. Rum was a big deal because of one word: money. Rum was a major export of the colonies. So, not a good time to be open supporters of the Brits in New Jersey, either.

The Leedses were already loathed for their British sympathies; now they had a son back from the dead (according to Ben Franklin), a dad labeled the Devil's messenger (according to the neighborhood Quakers), and a family crest covered in dragons. *Maybe there is something to the idea that they are associated with secret evil*, you could imagine some colonial neighbor thinking upon finding his butter soured in the churn and looking for someone to blame. It's no coincidence, either, that the Leeds Devil's birth aligns pretty closely with Titan Leeds's actual death in 1738. There is, however, no explanation for why Mother Leeds, who was married to neither Daniel nor Titan, ended up taking the brunt of the blame for the actions of the men of the family she had the great misfortune of marrying into. As if birthing and raising twelve non-devil kids hadn't been hard enough!

By the time the Revolutionary War began in 1775, the "Leeds Devil" had secured its place as a symbol of ridicule in a fledgling America. But while the political controversy around it died down by the nineteenth century, the story itself persisted. And somewhere along the line, the idea that the whole thing arose from a bunch of townsfolk picking on an unpopular family was lost and only the scary Satan stuff remained. Over the years, magazines like the

Atlantic Monthly printed versions of the folk tale involving curses, witchcraft, satanism, and monsters.[150] In 1910, the Arch Museum of Philadelphia[151] advertised the appearance of the devil in broad daylight, which the museum manager claimed to have personally captured. In fact, the "Devil" was just a stuffed kangaroo with wings sewn on, and the museum closed for good a few weeks later. Nevertheless, it was around that time that the "Leeds Devil" began to be known as the "Jersey Devil."

IT'S A REAL HOOT

So what is the Jersey Devil, really?

Well, when you put all these descriptions together, as fantastical animals go, the Jersey Devil may look something like Charizard, but sound more like a Creeper. How evil is it? If you graphed it with all the *Minecraft* mobs, it would be situated more firmly within the wicked quadrant of a Warden than that of an adorable Allay. Whatever its exact position on this made-up spectrum, the fact remains that something is almost certainly out there in those ancient stretches of pine forest. And the likeliest culprit, believe it

....

[150] So it must be true!

[151] The sworn enemy of the Museum of Philadelphia. Ha ha. Google it to track down the official name and you'll get: Arch Street Museum, Arch Dime Museum, Arch Street Dime Museum. See why fact-checking is a thing? Can folks not cut and paste properly? Are they all different museums? Or did one museum really have that many different names (and an identity complex)?

or not, is the great horned owl, aka *Bubo virginianus*, which is also an awesome name for a band that features a steel guitar and probably a mandolin.

At first blush, you wouldn't think an owl fits with the giant monster that has been described over the centuries by eyewitnesses like Joseph Bonaparte. But when you consider that before the invention of flashlights, most people had never seen this nocturnal bird up close and personal,[152] and then you take those meaty bits and throw them in a nice pot and combine them with a good description of the owl's body parts and behaviors, things start to make a little more sense. More sense than a flying llama, at least.

Here's a description of said owl, cobbled together from various resources to give you a better idea of what we're talking about. The great horned owl is a "savage and powerful nocturnal raptor" that flies virtually noiselessly with a nearly five-foot wingspan. It has big, round yellow eyes that stare out unblinkingly from under a set of feather tufts called plumicorns that function like eyebrows but look like horns. It strikes from above and uses its powerful talons—which are the largest of any owl species as a proportion of body size—to carry away animals several times its size. It's been known to scoop up dogs, cats, rabbits, foxes, even the occasional porcupine; and to bend these poor woodland and household creatures to its will,

....
[152] Josh saw a bunch of owls up close and personal when he went to an owl café once in Tokyo. It was a hoot (sorry).

it uses those strong, oversized talons to crush and sever their spines. Their young beg with a hissing scream. Oh, and it will also hunt for smaller game by walking along the ground.

To the uninitiated and the nyctophobic,[153] the great horned owl was nightmare fuel. To the religious and superstitious, of which there were many when Jersey Devil sightings were at their peak, that nightmare was real, because the owl has been a Christian symbol of death and a manifestation

[153] Fear of the dark is called nyctophobia.

of Satan since medieval times.[154] Is it any wonder, then, when you add in the natural human instinct to exaggerate when frightened or under duress, that a bright-eyed, sharp-beaked bird of prey with oversized talons, feathers that look like horns, and a wingspan wider than a carriage might get mistaken for a satanic monster puked from the depths of hell when it descends silently out of the darkness to release a terrifying, ear-piercing screech?

We say it is no wonder at all. But if you're curious (and brave) enough to find out for certain, you could venture into the Pine Barrens to look for yourself.[155] We're sure the National Park Service would be eternally grateful because it probably is, like Jersey's own Bon Jovi says, wanted dead or alive.[156]

....

[154] The Dutch Renaissance painter Hieronymus Bosch painted depictions of countless religious scenes and stories and was well-known for including owls in most of his work. Honestly, though, what animal hasn't been suspected of being Satan since medieval times? Llamas have probably even been included in that bunch. We would guess especially flying llamas.

[155] Before venturing to the Pine Barrens in search of the Jersey Devil, please sign and return the waiver form printed at the back of this book, releasing *Stuff Kids Should Know*, its successors, heirs, subsidiaries, and affiliates from any liability should any misfortune befall you during your Jersey Devil hunt (i.e., being attacked by a great horned owl). If your copy of *Stuff Kids Should Know: The Mind-Blowing Histories of (Almost) Everything* was published without the Jersey Devil Waiver Form, or if you'd just like to get your free catalog, please write to: Consumer Information Catalog, Pueblo, Colorado 81009.

[156] It's not. It's really, really not.

~~~~~~

CHAPTER 10

TRILLIONAIRES

ARE THEY POSSIBLE, AND WHO WILL IT BE?

1,000,000,000,000. That is a trillion. A one followed by twelve zeros. It's so long it looks like a freight train with the 1 as the locomotive. A trillion is one of those figures that's so immense it feels more like an idea than an actual amount.

One trillion feels easier to calculate than to conceptualize—like imagining the length of a light-year or the width of an atomic nucleus or the whip of a derby whiplash. That's the crazy part about a number like a trillion: It only shows up naturally on a scale of the infinitely large or the infinitesimally small.

So, hold on to your abaci, because we're about to break your brain. There are 100 trillion atoms in a single human cell, and there are about 70 trillion cells in a single human body. But if you add up the weight of all the human bodies (people) in the world, it would come to less than a trillion pounds,[157] though it would still be more than the combined

....

[157] This isn't nearly as impressive when converted to kilograms, as one trillion pounds equals 454,545,454,545.4545 kg. That's an interesting number, sure, but I think we can all agree that the imperial system of measurement trumps metric here again.

weight of all 1,000 trillion ants that live on Earth. God knows what this is in Big Macs.

Astronomers estimate there are 2 trillion galaxies in the universe, composed of a trillion trillion stars. One light-year is 5.88 trillion miles,[158] and the closest star to Earth beyond the sun is 4.25 light-years away: That's 25 trillion miles if you're counting, which you shouldn't be, because if you're counting at one number per second (which is very generous) it would take you a shade over 790,000 years to finish.[159]

YOU GET A TRILLION. YOU GET A TRILLION!

A trillion doesn't get any more comprehensible when we're talking about money either. A trillion US dollars is just shy of Mexico's entire GDP,[160] for example. It would take the average American family 16 million years to earn it and 2.73 million years to spend it at $1,000 per day. And if you wanted to stack it all in one place so you could see it, you'd need a stadium and a stepladder, because $1 trillion laid out neatly in $100 bills would produce stacks that cover

---

[158] That's 9,462,942,720,000 kilometers. This one is a wash, since both numbers are very impressive and interesting-looking.

[159] Even David Sinclair would agree there's not enough NMN on this planet to extend human lifespan that far (see Chapter 6).

[160] GDP is not the same as what goes into their piggy bank. Gross domestic product is how much $ the things and services that are produced are worth. Mexico's GDP in 2018 was USD$1.221 trillion.

nearly an entire football field at 10 feet high.[161] Make it $1 bills and you're looking at a mound of money roughly the size of the Empire State Building. And the size in Big Macs? Again, who knows?

So how is it that we could even be talking about the idea of one person in possession of such an unfathomable amount of cash? Is that really possible? The short answer is yes ...

... with about 89.7 sextillion asterisks,[162] because that was the effective inflation rate in Zimbabwe at the end of 2008. At its worst, the hyperinflation in Zimbabwe's currency rendered one US dollar worth 2,621,984,228,675,650, 147,435,579,309,984,228 Zimbabwe dollars. At that point pretty much every Zimbabwean became a de facto trillionaire, a fact that the Reserve Bank of Zimbabwe made official in 2009 when they rang in the new year by putting a whole suite of trillion-dollar notes (10, 50, and 100) into circulation. Not that you could buy much with them. When the story of the trillion-dollar notes broke that January, a loaf of bread cost Z$300 billion and the price wasn't heading anywhere good.[163]

Obviously when we talk about the possibility of trillionaires,

....

[161] 3.048 meters; yawn.

[162] There is no metric conversion for asterisks, but a sextillion is a thousand raised to the seventh power. Go ask a math teacher.

[163] Zimbabwe officially discontinued their trillion-dollar notes and abandoned their own currency for the US dollar in 2015. Locals could get USD$5 for every Z$175 quadrillion (that's 16 zeros) they turned in. You can hear all about this economic chaos in our episode "How Currency Works" (and we're pretty sure it makes an appearance in our "How much money is in the world?" and "What is stagflation?" episodes too).

we don't mean by the measure of just any currency. In certain countries at certain times, like Zimbabwe in 2009, being a trillionaire can be pretty doable. One trillion Iranian rials isn't even USD$25 million, for example. And the top 21 richest people in the world today would all be trillionaires if their USDs were converted to Mexican pesos. But since the

US dollar is considered the world's currency, it is the currency upon which any consistent measure of wealth would have to be based. When you look at it like that, the conversation about trillionairity[164] starts to get much smaller and

----

[164] It's technically not a word, but it totally should be.

more specific, though not without first navigating through the ever-growing list of world billionaires.

WHO WANTS TO BE A TRILLIONAIRE?

At one time it was generally believed that John D. Rockefeller, the guy who once controlled 90 percent of the oil business in the US, was the first billionaire. His net worth has since been disputed by his own son, and even though his inflation-adjusted wealth would still rank him somewhere on most reputable[165] All-Time Top Ten Richest Persons lists, Henry Ford has firmly supplanted the Standard Oil titan as the first true-blue billionaire.

Whether you ride with the guy who built the cars or the guy who put the gas in them, the billionaire seal was broken long before most of us were born, which means we all grew up knowing that making Richie Rich money was possible, if highly improbable.[166] This fueled our fascination with extreme wealth. We love shows like *Lifestyles of the Rich and Famous* and *Keeping Up with the Kardashians*, and we eat up that stuff like the Forbes 400 list.

There's even one list of the richest people of all time that has the Soviet Union leader Joseph Stalin at number 5.[167]

---

[165] "Reputable" being a relative term here.

[166] Chuck's favorite comic was *Richie Rich* and he stands by that.

[167] Stalin may have only been the fifth wealthiest ever, but he had a Top Three Walrus mustache.

That might seem like cheating—maybe not worth a septillion asterisks, but at least one—because Stalin wasn't personally wealthy. He didn't have a fortune invested in stocks. He wasn't an oil man or an industrialist or an entrepreneur, either. What he did have was complete authority over a country whose economy made up 9.6 percent of the globe's GDP. That is a staggering amount of wealth, no matter who wields it, and by the standard of any time period, and we would be remiss not to include him. We wouldn't want to hurt Stalin's feelings.

The reality is, if we're going to imagine a world in which trillionaires are possible, we have to consider all the ways that could happen, from Powerball winners to power-hungry dictators. It may not be as fun to imagine a murderous tyrant becoming a trillionaire as, say, a late-night-tweeting Elon Musk. But let's not kid ourselves: Andrew Carnegie, who ranked fourth on one of those most reputable lists, once hired a militia that killed nine striking workers. Bill Gates, who ranked ninth on that same list, may be a grandfatherly, world-saving guy now, but in his prime he was ruthless, gawky, and in control of a monopoly. If we're really going to entertain the idea of someone becoming a trillionaire when nearly half the world lives on less than $6 a day, then we also have to accept that it probably won't come pretty. And when we look at history, that's exactly what we find.

Of the top ten all-time richest people, two were conquerors who plowed their way across the globe to amass vast fortunes; two were industry owners who gained monopolies over critical resources and maintained control with force and cunning; five were dictator-emperors who held absolute authority over a global superpower; and one was a software developer who gained a monopoly over the personal computer industry and used laws to amass a personal fortune.

ABOUT RULERS

Stalin rubs elbows with other historic rulers whose nations' economies were one and the same as their personal wealth. Augustus Caesar personally owned Egypt for a time; India's Akbar I, who ruled the Moghul empire in the sixteenth century, had an economy comparable to Elizabethan England's; and the thirteenth- and fourteenth-century ruler of the Kingdom of Timbuktu, Mansa Musa, is—due to his nation's gold mines—considered perhaps the wealthiest person to have ever lived. There is a tale that when Musa passed through Egypt during a pilgrimage to Mecca, his incredible spending so flooded the market with gold that he temporarily reduced the value of Egypt's currency. That, friends, is how you make it rain in the desert.

It stands to reason, then, that at some point in the past the functional equivalent of a trillionaire has probably already walked the Earth; there just weren't USDs around to use as a measure of their wealth. And whoever becomes the first technical trillionaire won't look awfully different from those who've come before them. They will probably be something of a dictator or dominate a monopoly—if not literally, then figuratively—and utilize some combination of strategies and tactics that have already proven effective.[168]

This leaves us with two people who've got a legitimate

....
[168] We've grown depressed enough with this question that we now wonder why we asked it in the first place.

shot at being the first to ride that twelve-zero freight train to Trillionaire Town: Vladimir Putin and Jeff Bezos.

Rootin' Tootin' Shootin' Putin has maintained total control over Russia's USD$1.6 trillion GDP since 2000. His personal fortune—which he totally earned fair and square, in case the FSB is reading this—is somewhere between $200 to $300 billion[169] according to American and British intelligence reports. But given the invisibility cloak that Putin operates behind, his true wealth will probably never be known.[170]

Not to be outdone is Jeff Bezos, who is the world's richest private citizen by a comfortable margin and the founder of Amazon, which has effectively swallowed up all companies in its way and has its sights set on pretty much everything that could find its way inside your house, business, car, and body. Even if you opt to stick it to the man (Bezos) and you don't use Amazon or shop at Whole Foods (which Amazon bought for a mere $13 billion), you are still a cog in the Bezos Empire if you have an account with Netflix, Twitter, Facebook, Twitch, Reddit, and too many other platforms to name because they all run on Amazon Web Services, far and away the largest and most relied-upon cloud service in the world.[171] If you aren't

....

[169] And that is not in Zimbabwe dollars.

[170] If someone does put all the pieces together, they better watch out, because a nice, warm slice of polonium pie is headed their way.

[171] Not uneasy yet? Check out our episode "How AI Facial Recognition Works," which talks about how Amazon Web Services powers the tracking systems of the world's police and governments.

even on social media, this is still Jeff Bezos's world and you're just living in it. Listen closely on a quiet night, you can sometimes hear his "mmmwuhhahahaha" carried thinly on the breeze.

By some calculations, Bezos could be the first member of the Trillionaire's Club by 2026, but a lot would have to go right and stay right for that to happen, and even Bezos doesn't think that's likely, having once pointed out that large companies typically last thirty years, not the hundred-or-more-year timeline you can imagine would ease a billionaire comfortably into trillionairehood. Based on that prediction, Amazon will start to fail somewhere around 2024, its thirtieth birthday—two years before Bezos would hit a trillion, if everything were to continue as it has been going. So sad.

But as much money as Bezos can make from his Amazon apparatus here on Earth, it may likely be space rocks that ultimately tip the scale on his balance sheets. Renowned astrophysicist Neil deGrasse Tyson once triumphantly declared, "It is likely that the first trillionaire will be the person who exploits the mineral resources on asteroids." Well guess what: Jeff Bezos founded a space exploration company called Blue Origin to eventually do just that.

According to Asterank, a database that tracks asteroid contents and value, there are several hundred asteroids in our solar system, each with more than $100 trillion worth of minerals and rare earth metals trapped inside them. That's more than the combined GDP of our entire planet . . . in one flying space rock.[172]

Both Putin and Bezos are conquerors in their own ways. But only one has a shirtless picture of himself riding a horse[173] on vacation in Siberia, which probably gives him the upper hand on the race to twelve zeros.

---

[172] Of course, if Bezos was able to successfully wrangle, mine, and bring to market the mineral contents of an asteroid, we'd immediately be in a Mansa Musa situation where the value of everything starts to collapse. Still, though . . . a hundred trillion dollars!

[173] Putin is kind of famous for stunts—petting a polar bear in the Arctic (of course it was staged), saving a crew from a tiger (conveniently not caught on camera), parading his bare chest in front of cameras—to pump up his popularity. Good luck with that.

CHAPTER 11

THE SCOTLAND YARD CRIME MUSEUM

NOTHING TO SEE HERE

In London, on the first floor of the New Scotland Yard, officially the headquarters for the Metropolitan Police Service, there is a place you can go to learn everything you could ever want to know about the most famous crimes and criminals in Britain and all the cool old-timey ways they did their dirt, got caught, and were punished.

Actually, that's not true. You can't go there. Or, we should say, you can't go there.[174] The Scotland Yard Crime Museum, or the "Black Museum," as it has been more popularly

....

[174] Got it now?

known over the decades, is closed to the public.[175] Instead, it functions more like a private reference library for British police—a classical training tool for becoming better Sherlock and Enola Holmeses.

Video surveillance? DNA analysis? Advanced interrogation techniques? Sure, these modern crime-fighting methods are technically responsible for solving most homicide cases these days, and you can learn them if you want, but they won't help you as a copper or a detective inspector when you need to know from a distance what an umbrella shotgun looks like (it looks awesome, FYI), or how to tell by weight how many eightpenny common nails are inside a suitcase bomb (a lot), or know by the shape and feel of a murderer's skull whether they were born a criminal or made into one (more on this later).

For that, you gotta go old-school. You gotta get your hands on some history. You gotta go to the Black Museum.

BLACK MUSEUM: ORIGINS

The Black Museum began with the opening of the Central Prisoners Property Store in April 1874. Soon thereafter it

....

[175] According to popular lore, the "Black Museum" got its name from an 1877 *Observer* article when a reporter doing a story on the place was denied entry, but it seems more likely that the name was taken from this line in the piece: "The building is, indeed, as it is called, a Black Museum, for it is associated with whatever is darkest in human nature."

unofficially became a museum thanks to an Inspector Percy Neame, who got the bright idea to train the Metropolitan Police's new recruits in burglary detection by putting together a selection of tools they'd taken off convicted burglars.[176] Neame's home invasion show-and-tell must have been quite the hit, because within a year his collection of criminal artifacts would expand well beyond burglary, and the place where he displayed them would get the seal of approval as an actual museum. Its doors would soon open to British law enforcement, and for the next 100 years, as if on the lam, the museum would move several times when both the collection and its home, Met HQ, outgrew their previous spaces.

STUFF YOU SHOULD KNOW . . .

ABOUT LANGUAGE

Scotland Yard is home to London's Metropolitan Police and to a crime museum that no one gets to visit, but it's something else too. It's a metonym.

A metonym is a term with its own separate meaning that is also used as a stand-in to describe something to which

---

[176] Victorian society was fascinated by seedy characters who lurked in dark corners, burglars foremost among them. They fill the pages of novels from the Victorian period as both heroes and villains alike—it's like Netflix before there was Netflix.

it is closely related. Hollywood is a section of Los Angeles, for example, but it is also a substitute term for the entertainment industry. The crown is something the queen wears, but it is also used to mean the queen herself. A gun is a thing used to commit a crime, but in hired gun it is used to mean the person who uses the gun. That makes each of these terms a metonym.

Scotland Yard is the name for the original entrance to the Metropolitan Police headquarters. When it eventually became the substitute name for the London police as a whole, it became a metonym.

While the idea for the museum began in 1874, seven years into Neame's tenure with the Met,[177] what made this particular museum possible in the first place was a piece of legislation passed by Parliament a few years earlier, called the Prisoners Property Act of 1869.

The Prisoners Property Act apparently did two things: It required police to hold on to a prisoner's property once they were convicted, then return it to them upon their release;[178] and it subsequently gave police the right to keep a prisoner's

[177] Percy Neame would stay with the Met for another 28 years and retire as the superintendent of the Criminal Investigation Department in 1902. That turned out to be a big year for Superintendent Neame, as he died in 1902 as well.

[178] This is what precipitated the creation of the Central Prisoners Property Store in the first place.

property and to use it for instructional purposes if the property was abandoned by recently freed prisoners—or, as was more often the case with the property that has made its way into the Black Museum, the prisoner no longer needed their stuff because they'd been executed.

The Met's collection of crime memorabilia captured the imagination of the British public almost immediately. Too bad for the general public since they would never get a chance to look inside—the museum's contents have not been accessible for public viewing except for one single six-month joint exhibition with the Museum of London from 2015 to 2016.[179] But an odd smattering of famous people was given tours within the first 30 or 40 years of the museum's existence, including George V and various members of the British royal family, Harry Houdini, Laurel and Hardy, and Sir Arthur Conan Doyle—crime-crazed ghouls, every last one of them.

----

[179] The fact that this particular six-month period was the only time in history the museum allowed the public to browse a sample of its keepsakes is bad enough, but what makes it worse, at least for us, is that we performed live in London in July 2016, just three months after the exhibition closed. So out of the more than 280 six-month periods that make up the museum's entire history, it's been open for just one of those. And out of the 560 three-month periods in the museum's history, the one we show up to London for is the one that comes immediately after the single six-month period the museum's collection was on display. Cursed!

A LOOK INSIDE
THE "MUSEUM"

This inaccessibility brings up an interesting question, though: Like the sound of a tree falling in the forest with no one around to hear it, is a collection of stuff really a museum if no one is allowed to look at it? Doesn't the fact that only members of a specific group (British law enforcement) have access mean this place is more like an archive or, worse, some ghastly trophy case?

Maybe we're just being pedantic because we really, really, really want to get inside this place, and it sucks that we can't just buy tickets at the entrance and a T-shirt as we exit through the gift shop. Museums aren't supposed to be private institutions of instruction (those are called schools)— they're supposed to be houses of inspiration available to all crime-crazed ghouls. And that's not just our opinion: It says so right there in the name!

The word *museum* is derived from the ancient Greek *mouseion*, meaning "seat of the muses." As anybody who's a fan of Percy Jackson knows, the muses were the goddesses of arts and science, the source of all knowledge, in Greek mythology. In modern times they're thought of mostly as sources of creativity and artistic inspiration, occasionally depicted on roller skates. In a way, you could say that the museum as a concept is their physical legacy and—*dang it just let us in so we can see all the death masks!*

What's that? Death masks, you say? Oh yes, death masks. Masks o' death. Read on for more . . .

DEATH MASKS ARE COOL

Setting aside for a moment whether or not the Scotland Yard Black Museum is, in fact, a museum, what's indisputable is that the place is full of some amazingly cool and interesting things:

- **A pair of bandits' masks, perhaps the lamest ever (see the sadly accurate illustration seen above), which belonged to Albert and Alfred Stratton, the first British criminals to be convicted of murder on the strength of fingerprint evidence.**

- **Three gallstones that were all that remained of Olive Durand-Deacon after her body was dissolved in acid by John Haigh in 1949, and which helped convict Haigh.**

- Super creepy stuff like a cup made from a skull, a pickled brain, and a hand—just the bones.

- An arsenal of weaponry, from knives and guns to dynamite-filled bombs and a poison-filled syringe belonging to the Kray Brothers,[180] which we guess you could call tools of the murder trade.

- Tools of various other trades, such as counterfeiters, burglars, spies—including a can opener, a cook pot, and a shopping bag, none of which seem evil until you let your mind wander to the ways a murderer might use them.

But coolest of all, judging from pictures at least—since we're not allowed to go inside—are a series of death masks belonging to some of Britain's most notorious criminals, all of them mounted high up on the walls like hunting trophies.[181]

Death masks are nothing new, to be clear. As a matter of fact, they've been around since the ancient Egyptians.[182] Initially, at least in the case of the Egyptians, they were

....

[180] Reggie and Ronnie Kray were immortalized in the Morrissey song "The Last of the Famous International Playboys" and were played by real-life brothers Gary and Martin Kemp from the band Spandau Ballet in a British movie called *The Krays*, and also played simultaneously by Tom Hardy in a movie called *Legend*.

[181] While they were certainly not intended to be viewed as celebratory mementos, it's not hard to imagine British police officers touring the museum, looking up at all the death masks around them, and vigorously shaking their fists at each other (aka the British High-Five) as if to say "Huzzah, ol' chap, we got the dastardly buggers!" Or something very British like that.

[182] Perhaps the world's most famous death mask is also one of the great masterpieces of Egyptian art. It is King Tutankhamun's death mask, discovered by Egyptologist Howard Carter.

fashioned to fit over the face of the dead as part of elaborate funeral rituals so that the soul of the deceased could recognize and rejoin its body in the afterlife.

Starting in the Middle Ages, however, death masks evolved into more literal representations of the dead. They were created shortly after death, usually with some kind of wax or plaster material applied directly to the person's face, in order to create the most accurate visage possible. Typically, they were created as molds for sculptors or for use as funeral effigies or on tombs, and over time they became valuable pieces of art in themselves.

Their real heyday, though, was the eighteenth and nineteenth centuries, when everyone who was anyone had a death mask made. Sir Isaac Newton has one. Napoleon has one. So many famous composers have death masks—Mozart, Haydn, and Schubert among them—that the Vienna Funeral Museum was able to build an entire exhibition around them in 2020 to celebrate the 250th birthday of Ludwig van Beethoven . . . who has two death masks.

It's not immediately clear why death masks became so popular—they were like the leggings of the Romantic Age, except for your dead face instead of your dancin' legs—but their increasing use by scientists in emerging fields of study at that time almost certainly had something to do with it. It is definitely a big part of why the Black Museum's death masks are so interesting.

PHRENOLOGY: THE SCIENCE OF THOSE BUMPS ON YOUR HEAD

There are two things (stuffs) you should know about the Black Museum's death mask collection: First, most if not all of them came from London's notorious Newgate Prison upon its closure in 1902,[183] and second, they're not actually masks. Unlike most death masks from earlier periods, which stop behind the ears, these masks are actually full 360-degree casts of the heads of executed criminals dating back to the late 1830s. They were commissioned, ostensibly, for the purpose of studying the size and shape of the skulls—a pseudoscience, though it was not considered quite so pseudo back then, called phrenology.

It's simplest to describe phrenology as the study of the mind from the outside. It involves measuring all the bumps and dents and protrusions you'll find on any given person's skull and using them as an indicator of the quality of various structures that comprise the brain. Phrenologists believed that each of the 27 structures was the seat of certain mental

---

[183] According to one of the curators at the Museum of London who organized the 2015–2016 joint exhibition with the Black Museum that we missed by a mere three months, a number of the masks were once displayed by the governor of Newgate Prison at his home. Charles Dickens (who wrote *A Christmas Carol*, the book that has been made into a movie ten times!) even saw a couple of them when he visited the prison in 1836.

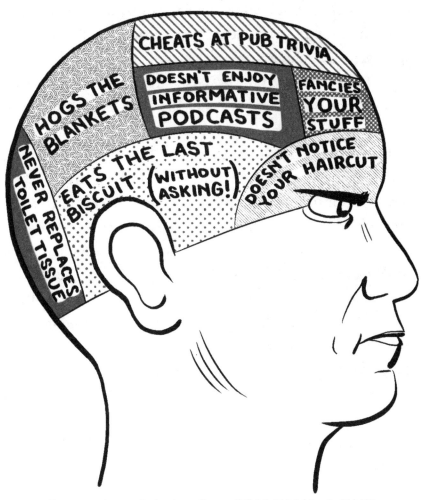

CHEATS AT PUB TRIVIA

DOESN'T ENJOY INFORMATIVE PODCASTS

FANCIES YOUR STUFF

HOGS THE BLANKETS

NEVER REPLACES TOILET TISSUE

EATS THE LAST BISCUIT

(WITHOUT ASKING!)

DOESN'T NOTICE YOUR HAIRCUT

PHRENOLOGY of a CRIMINAL MIND

traits. In theory, a large bump meant the structure of the brain under that section of skull was bigger, and therefore its associated traits were more noticeable. An indentation, in contrast, usually meant a weakness in that area of the brain. Nice and tidy and scientific-like.

Prisoners became a valuable resource for phrenologists for two reasons, one practical and one theoretical. Practically, they were an abundant, condemned, renewable population.[184] Theoretically, they were ripe for evaluation because they all had something in common—they were criminals. And if phrenologists (i.e., quacks) could discover some dent or bump common to all of Newgate Prison's late residents' death masks, they might be able to isolate the area of the brain responsible for antisocial, criminal behavior. Not to mention the Criminal Indentation (or the Crooks' Dent, as we've just now decided to call it)[185] might also function as a baseline for measurements related to other behaviors. Why, you could go around feeling people's heads and lock up the ones you find with the Crooks' Dent for life—before they could carry out a single crime! Perfectly logical!

Now, this idea that the brain has different parts that are responsible for different actions or behaviors—a concept called "localization of function"—isn't so crazy. It would ultimately be proven true in 1861 when pioneering French neurosurgeon Paul Broca[186] proved the existence of the brain's

[184] A quite dehumanizing position, but a socially accepted attitude at the time.

[185] This is an astounding amount of creative license we've taken here. Not only did we create a slang term, Crooks' Dent, but we made up the term it's derived from, Criminal Indentation, as well!

[186] Broca's area (BA) made a number of appearances earlier in *SYSK* episode history when we talked about things related to language. BA is a great guest star, one of the all-time class acts. BA would clean up the greenroom while waiting, always tipped Jeri, and one time brought us all really nice watches as host gifts. We'd have BA back anytime.

speech center. So, it's pretty interesting that the guy who first proposed the very correct localization of function theory back in 1796, a German physician named Franz Joseph Gall, was also the father of the very incorrect field of phrenology— whose 27 structures, their association to specific traits like the Crooks' Dent, and every bit of the skullreadery involved all turned out to be total bunk.[187]

The Scotland Yard Black Museum and phrenology have a lot in common in this way. There's only so much you can learn about what's on the inside when you can only take a look at it from the outside. No matter how sensitive the contents, if you want to know the truth, eventually you're going to need access. Hint, hint.

----

[187] The product of an overactive imagination, which undoubtedly resided within a part of Gall's brain that sat under a section of skull that had a big ol' knot on it.

~~~~~~~~~~~~~~~~~~~~~~~~~~~~~~~~

CHAPTER 12

WELL-WITCHING

THE ANCIENT ART OF GUESSING WITH A STICK

Every March in Tanzania, 1.5 million wildebeests, along with another half-million zebras and antelopes, begin tracing an invisible 1,800-mile elliptical circuit that moves clockwise from the southern Serengeti, northwesterly through the Upper Grumeti River woodlands, into Kenya's Masai Mara and back again, following the rains in pursuit of fresh grasslands.

At some point in spring a few wildebeests simply get up and start walking.

A couple million animals just sort of agree now's as good a time as any and start following the leaders. A few months later, in June and July, at the start of the dry season, some herds of African savannah elephants who share the region with the wildebeests also begin their long, ever-shifting treks in search of more reliable sources of water and abundant vegetation.[188]

These annual migrations have likely been going on for millions of years, and the whole thing has a certain mystical quality to it. It's possible the traveling wildebeests begin their trek based on changing levels of phosphorus and nitrogen in the grass that vary with the wet or dry seasons. Or maybe it's just a million years of survival instinct coded into their DNA. Elephant herds, for their part, rely on the remarkable memories of their matriarchs to get moving, as well as an intricate set of senses and behaviors (vibrations, touch, chemical secretions, specific gestures) to pass along information to the rest of the herd about where they're headed.[189] And while scientists haven't pinpointed exactly how these migrations occur or what triggers them to start, what they do know (or at least suspect) is that there are a number of deeply ingrained evolutionary processes at work, all guiding the animals' fundamental search for water.

Then there's us (humans). We've been around for 200,000 years—50,000 if you're only counting modern humans like

---

[188] While all the wildebeests in East Africa tend to migrate, not all savannah elephants do. A 2018 study revealed that only 25 percent of elephants reliably migrate. The rest kind of do whatever they want, which we suppose is to be expected from the largest land mammal on Earth.

[189] Elephants don't only know where to go, they know where not to go. They can carry mental "Do Not Enter" signs attached to specific locations for generations, only to take those signs down when the coast is clear, even though the elephants who first sensed the danger are long dead. As you may already know from our episode "Elephants: The Best Animals?," elephants are incredible.

you and me—and we have an evolutionary lineage that stretches millions of years further back than that. And yet, for at least the last 8,000 of those years, when we've gone searching for water during droughts and dry seasons, we haven't relied on evolutionary instinct, or heightened olfactory ability, or a finely tuned taste for phosphorus, or sounds or scratching or touch. We've just used a stick.

Locating groundwater with a stick has been given different names over the centuries: water-finding, water-dowsing, water-witching, willow-witching, well-witching.[190] So much witching. But whatever the name, the practice is, at its core, a process whereby the holder of the stick predicts the location of an underground water source based solely on the movement of a stick in their hands as they walk the land.

H₂OVER THERE!

Here's how the process is traditionally supposed to work. First, an aspiring well-witcher cuts a branch from a tree.[191] Not just any branch, but one that is naturally forked in a Y shape, with each of the three segments ideally measuring

[190] Quite a few synonyms for something that, spoiler alert, doesn't actually seem to be real.

[191] It doesn't appear to matter what kind of tree the branch comes from, but willow trees, witch hazel, and fruit trees, particularly peach trees, seem to be the most popular. Willows certainly make sense because their presence indicates an underground water source is nearby and relatively near the surface. Or it could just be that they're popular because they're very pretty.

between twelve and sixteen inches, then trimmed of smaller twigs and leaves so that the stem of the Y is as smooth as possible. Now the limb is no longer a useless branch but is called a dowsing rod, ready to find water for its maker.

The well-witcher then grabs the forked ends of the dowsing rod with a loose underhanded grip, like they're using an extra-wide game controller, and holds the rod parallel to the ground as they walk slowly across the terrain, visualizing the water beneath its surface. According to the *Farmers' Almanac*, maintaining a loose grip is an important part of the dowsing process because as you approach water the rod will begin to angle toward the earth, so you need to give it enough slack to do that. But not too much! When you get really close, the rod will point down sharply, and you want to maintain control of it . . . for reasons that are not at all clear.

If this sounds like a bit of an inexact science, that's because it isn't exactly science. Like phrenology, it is considered a pseudoscience by many. Other, less charitable types prefer the more technical term "total nonsense."

For instance, the National Groundwater Association, or the NGWA as it's known by all the cool kids in science class, opposes the use of "water witches" because "controlled experimental evidence clearly indicates that the technique is totally without scientific merit." Well, okay then, when you put it like that.

THE DURABILITY OF DOWSING

Except it's not quite that simple. Water-witching, or dowsing, which is the more general term for the practice, has been around for thousands of years, spanning the entire known world. It's depicted in cave paintings in the Sahara desert that date back to at least 6000 BCE (Before Common Era). Prehistoric Peruvian peoples did it. The Egyptians were doing it in 3000 BCE, and Moses and the Hebrews were doing it a thousand years after that as they fled from Egypt. In between, it showed up on the statue of a Chinese emperor and in the writings of Confucius. Over the next 2,000 years it made an appearance in Homer's epic poem *The Odyssey* as "the caduceus";[192] on the isle of Crete with the Oracle of Delphi; and in ancient Rome, where Cicero wrote about the use of a dowsing rod, which he called a *virgula divinatorium*. In the sixth century, the Indian mathematician Varahamihira included all sorts of information about "water divining" in

....

[192] The caduceus is the symbol of two snakes intertwined around a staff, with wings at the top, which tends to be (incorrectly) associated with doctors. The caduceus isn't the symbol for doctors, it's the symbol of the god Mercury, or Hermes, the messenger, who also happens to be the patron god of thieves and outlaws, not doctors. The correct symbol for doctors is the Rod of Asclepius, who was the Greek god of physicians and whose symbol is a single snake coiled around a rod, no wings. Somewhere along the way, someone got sloppy and mixed these two up. Then no one bothered to check the facts. So the next time you notice your doctor using the caduceus instead of the Rod of Asclepius, you might want to take it as a sign that you should get a second opinion.

his Sanskrit encyclopedia, *Brihat Samhita*. By the middle of the sixteenth century, dowsing had witched its way fully across Europe, drawing the attention of religious figures like Martin Luther, who insisted it was the work of the Devil.

Of course that stopped it. Not! In the twentieth century, dowsing was studied intently by the English and the Germans, and in the Soviet Union, where it was called "biophysical locating" and you could actually get a degree in it.[193] Today, dowsing does not get that kind of official institutional recognition, but there are still plenty of dowsing societies all over the world. The biggest of them all, the American Society of Dowsers, has more than seventy-five local chapters. As far as we know, none of them are affiliated with the Devil.

One of the big reasons dowsing seems to have endured throughout history is that it doesn't just apply to water. It's also been used for hundreds, sometimes thousands, of years to find other valuable things buried in the ground: precious metals like gold, minerals and gemstones, and oil and natural gas foremost among them.[194] Legend has it that

---

[193] Trying to get a leg up on the US during the Cold War, the Soviets went in for all kinds of paranormal phenomena—stuff that can't be explained by science—like telepathy (reading other people's minds), clairvoyance (seeing into the future), and telekinesis (moving things with your mind).

[194] As we talked about in our episode on Project Stargate, the self-proclaimed clairvoyant and telekinetic Uri Geller has made quite a bit of money being hired by oil and mineral companies to find deposits by dowsing. Dowsing for oil in particular has its own name—doodle-bugging—coined by Americans, because next to Australians, only Americans can come up with words and phrases that give you no clue about the things they describe.

Cleopatra brought dowsers with her so they could search for gold wherever she went. And back in 1556, an illustration of mineral dowsing appears in *De Re Metallica*, the awesome title to Georgius Agricola's seminal text highlighting German mining and metallurgy.[195]

TOOLS OF THE DOWSING TRADE

Y-ROD 	The oldest type of dowsing tool, derived from the traditional tree branch, the Y-Rod bends toward the ground when water or something equally valuable is detected.
L-RODS 	These come in pairs and are held like six-shooters or VR controllers. In their earliest incarnations, when an underground substance was detected, the rods would cross in front of the dowser. Today, L-Rods also spin 360 degrees at the point where the long horizontal rod meets the short vertical handle (and, we like to imagine, make an excited "homina homina homina" sound).

[195] This is not, by the by, where the heavy metal band Metallica gets its name. That came from a guy named Ron Quintana, who drummer Lars Ulrich met at a party in San Francisco in 1981. Quintana asked Ulrich which name he thought would be best for a new metal fanzine (way before e-zines) that Quintana was creating—MetalMania or Metallica. Ulrich told Quintana to go with MetalMania, and then used Metallica himself.

WAND

One of the oldest dowsing tools, this is a four-foot-long tapered stick, also called a "bobber," that the dowser holds by the slender end and waits for a bobbing motion in the wand to indicate the presence of water.[196] Modern bobbers are smaller, with a handle and a thin, flexible rod with some kind of counterweight on the end of it.

PENDULUM

Dangled by hand over a physical area or even a map, it will begin to swing or spiral when it has detected something. As dowsing tools, pendulums are as old as, if not older than, Y-Rods. The Cairo Museum has a number of them on display that were removed from tombs that are thousands of years old.[197]

[196] Egyptian hieroglyphs describe a magic wand of sorts, called Ur-Heka, that was also used for dowsing and that translated to "great magical power (that) makes water to come forth."

[197] Dead bodies, death masks, now dowsing pendulums. These ancient Egyptian tombs can hold almost as much stuff as Mr. Potato Head's butt.

That type and level of interest continue to the present day and has extended beyond what is buried to include what has gone missing—wallets, keys, planes, and ships. There is a big market for custom dowsing rods designed specifically for finding ~~suckers~~ all manner of buried treasure and lost items.

In America there's a market for dowsing expertise among miners, prospectors, ranchers, and farmers who can't afford the more accurate (and much more expensive) geological surveys or test drilling that organizations like the NGWA recommend. Which probably helps explain why the NGWA felt the need to come out against dowsing with both water guns blazing: Dowsers are their competition. When money's tight, resources are scarce, and time is of the essence, the impulse is to get on the horn and call the guy with the biggest dowsing rod around.

WHAT'S REALLY (NOT) GOING ON?

Something like dowsing doesn't persist across the millennia or spread around the world unless there's something to it. If it were total nonsense, someone would have definitively disproved it by now, we'd have all had a good laugh, and it would become one of those little oddities from history that ends up as a *Jeopardy!* clue.[198] Like how we used to believe

---

[198] Or as a chapter in a book about random stuff you should know.

the sun revolved around the Earth, or that the speed and movement from riding on trains could cause people to go insane,[199] or that red meat and cigarettes were good for you. You'd think that's the conventional thinking anyway.

Alas, you'd be wrong, because here we are, knee-deep in the twenty-first century, with seventy-five separate dowsing clubs in the United States and an entire international network beyond them, all totally unaffiliated with the Devil and all ready to point us in the right direction toward water, wallets, or any manner of desirable things.

The issue is that the persistence of dowsing's existence does not disprove scientific studies, which have definitively disproved the effectiveness of dowsing for a number of decades now, as far back as the 1870s. According to numerous controlled studies since then, in fact, dowsers are no better than chance at detecting anything in the ground no matter what it is. And it's not exactly hard to find water hidden beneath the ground.

Something like 90 percent of Earth's surface has groundwater beneath it, and the NGWA says that the groundwater hidden out of view beneath the Earth's surface is 60 times more plentiful than surface freshwater deposits. Indeed, the last remaining bit of the mystery of dowsing—why a dowsing rod or a bobber or a pendulum moves in the hands of a

....

[199] The Victorian belief in "railway madness" was helped along by reports of agitated people removing their clothes, fighting with other passengers, and trashing passenger compartments, only to fully regain themselves when the train stopped once again.

dowser—can be explained not by what's in the ground, but rather what's in the dowser's mind.

This is called the "ideomotor effect." Normal unconscious activity or subconscious thoughts can produce slight but noticeable muscle movements that make it seem like whatever is in a person's hands at that moment is moving on its own, or in response to something outside their control.[200] The vast majority of dowsers honestly believe they are not moving the dowsing tool in their hands, and consciously they are not wrong. The mind can have a mind of its own sometimes.

Ironically, that is exactly the argument a dowser would make in support of dowsing's legitimacy. It's not actually about the rod or the wand or the pendulum, they will say, but the power of the human body to perceive and respond to the buried or missing material being sought. The rod is just an outward "indicator" that the person holding it has found something . . . with their mind. It's the ideomotor effect in reverse—or thrown back in your face, depending on your perspective.

Some dowsers believe all humans possess a kind of dowsing sixth sense that can be homed in on and sharpened with practice. Try it yourself and see if you've got it! Others have described a "dowsing reflex mechanism" that, it seems, has been tracked through brain waves by at least two researchers using EEGs when a dowser is dowsing. Here's how

....
[200] Yes, this is the phenomenon behind the "effectiveness" of Ouija boards as well.

Dr. Edith Jurka's 1980s research results were described in the updated third edition of *The Essential Dowsing Guide*, published in 2013:

When in the dowsing mode, the brainwave beta frequency of the thinking state lowers in frequency to the alpha state, which is a meditative state. When a dowsing target is found, there is a burst of the lower frequency theta state of around four to seven cycles per second, which corresponds to brainwave activity in dreaming sleep.

According to this idea, dowsing arises from a state of being entranced. Or as Edward Stillman, the scientific adviser to the American Dowsing Society, put it: "Dowsing appears to be a truly unique and creative altered state of human consciousness." One that requires us to abandon logic-dominated left brain thinking and to engage with the more sensitive right brain as much as possible so we might achieve that meditative state.

What would our right brains be sensing in this state? Well, in the case of water, at least, possibly the electromagnetic field and radio waves emitted by underground water running faster than two miles per hour. According to a British researcher named Alf Riggs, as the water passes through rock and sediment, it produces a "positive vertical electrical field," a "DC magnetic field," various radio frequencies, and both high-energy and ultrashort waves. This, the author of *The Essential Dowsing Guide* suggests, might be what some of the best dowsers and well-witchers are perceiving, and thus what their dowsing rods are responding to when they bend toward the earth, bob up and down, spiral around, or cross in front of them.

WHERE WE GO FROM HERE

Regular listeners of *Stuff You Should Know* may recognize that we seem to have traipsed pretty far into Rupert Sheldrake territory by this point.[201]

The idea that deposits of water can create disturbances within Earth's magnetic field certainly seems plausible.[202] And there are such things as alpha, beta, and theta brain waves. Perhaps most of all, the idea that humans have some innate sense that can pick up on these disturbances, which we can then use to find water hidden underground, is an attractive one. It has a certain sensibility; like the wildebeests, we too are products of natural selection, so a sense

....

[201] After our episode "How Morphic Fields Work?," Rupert Sheldrake has become *SYSK* shorthand for pseudoscientific stuff that sounds fairly convincing but upon closer inspection does not have any basis in current scientific understanding. This is not to say it's necessarily bunk, just that it may be bunk (probably is bunk). It is worth saying that we love minds like Rupert Sheldrake's; they make the world interesting and push science to look into areas outside its comfort zone. We believe scientific studies should be challenged, but we also tend to put stock in the scientific method.

[202] We found a cool paper from 1971 called "The Detection of Magnetic Fields Caused by Groundwater," by Utah State University's Duane G. Chadwick and Larry Jensen, that explains how it might work, but we didn't see much else on it. In no small part, we imagine, because since 1971 there have been significant technological advances in things like detection and electromagnetism.

like that would have contributed greatly to our survival as a species earlier in our evolutionary history. (Using that same sense to locate a lost wallet seems slightly more far-fetched.)

But as far as we can tell, no one's managed to successfully show in any reliable, repeatable way that humans—or even just some humans—have any kind of innate sense that would make us capable of dowsing. And almost all the studies that have been done have shown the opposite, that it does not seem to be a sense that humans possess.

Still, this one captured our imaginations and we don't feel good about poo-pooing it at this point. Perhaps the studies carried out thus far have been flawed in some way we aren't yet aware of. And it's become pretty clear that we have senses far more numerous than the standard five—who's to say we won't discover a sense for groundwater? Not us.

Maybe we should just let Occam and his trusty razor cut through the confusion instead. He usually has the simplest explanation, and it's almost always the right one. Or maybe we should look to the wildebeest and the savannah elephant of Africa, take to heart their ancient evolutionary wisdom, and, in the words of Atlanta's own TLC, stick to the rivers and lakes that we're used to. The trick is to still keep our minds open to finding hidden ones we haven't discovered yet.

CHAPTER 13

~~~~~~~~~~~~~~~~~~~~~~~~~~~~~~~~~~~~~~~

DOG SMELLS

CANINE SCENTS AND SENSE-ABILITY

One of the more underappreciated elements of director Christopher Nolan's dreamscape movie, *Inception*, is the way he depicts how action in the waking world can affect events in the dream world. A character is asleep inside a building that is under attack in the waking world, for example, and in the dream world everything starts crumbling around him.

We've probably all experienced a version of this in our own lives, even if we didn't realize it at the time. Next time you have a bad cold that makes it hard to breathe, don't be surprised if you wake up with a fright from a roller coaster dream or a falling dream, right at the start of the big drop, trying to catch your breath—that's how your lungs gasping for air in the waking world could translate in the dream world. Inception!

Not all real-world intrusions into our dreams are so dramatic or traumatic, however. Some are also delicious. Maybe you've had this dream: You're hungry. The mouth-watering smell of something salty and savory and warm is overwhelming your olfactory senses. You move toward it, but it seems to be eluding you, teasing you, until finally you see it. In your mind's eye it looks like a tray of nachos. Or maybe your grandma's Frito pie. The next thing you know, you're eating.

Crunch. Crunch. Crunch.

Suddenly, you begin to pick up steam, shoveling the food into your mouth. One bite, then another. No, wait.

Actually, someone is shoving it down your throat—it's like you're being waterboarded with a Fritos fire hose!

And that's when you wake up . . . to find your sleeping dog's outstretched paws in your face and their paw pads smelling distinctly like corn chips. If you don't own a dog, or if you are a monster who doesn't allow your dog to sleep with you,[203] this type of experience is likely quite foreign to you. Rest assured, it happens every day to permissive dog owners around the world and it smells yummy, which may be a big part of the reason dog owners don't do anything about it when they probably should.

FRITO FEET, QUITE THE COMBO

This phenomenon of a dog's paws smelling like corn chips is most popularly known as Frito Feet (or Toes). And while it would be comforting to believe that it only happens when

....

[203] Or if you're just a grown-up with good discipline and better hygiene.

the magical Corn Fairy sprinkles her special corn dust on all the good dogs each night, the reality is much mustier. That corn chip smell results from yeast and bacteria suspended within the moisture that gets caught between the pads of a dog's paws. How's that for a buzzkill?

The problem—and to be sure it can become a problem—starts with the fact that dogs only sweat where they don't have fur, so basically their noses and the bottoms of their paws.[204] And for some breeds, on their little pink "pig bellies." Then, when you take the ol' girl out for a walk, those sweaty pads inevitably come in contact with standing water, soil, and all manner of waste, each one a thriving breeding ground for a variety of bacteria and naturally occurring yeasts.

Once the bacteria and yeast are squeezed up between your dog's sweaty toes, they've found the perfect place to breed. It's dark, warm, damp, and protected by a carpeted canopy of fur. And, importantly, the area typically goes undisturbed so the microbes can get down to business munching dead skin and other miniature detritus. As they do their dirty business, they release volatile gases as waste products. It is

....

[204] The sweat produced in the paws and nose is largely meant to keep those areas from drying out and to release pheromones that act as chemical messengers to other animals (more on that later in the chapter). This kind of sweating does not help dogs regulate their temperature, however. For that, they turn to panting, which evaporates heat through their breath and cools them. They also use conduction to lower their temperature, like when their heat passes into a cool floor they are lying on. That's why so many dogs like to chill out in the kitchen or the bathroom. It's not because they're obsessed with food or poop, though both those things are true for many dogs. It's because those two rooms often have the coolest floors in the house.

those gases, not the bacteria or yeast themselves, that are largely responsible for the odor.

The particular odor all depends on the recipe—what is being digested, what kind of bacterium is doing the digesting, and what that digestion produces. In the right combination and proportions, that process can produce the unusual Frito Feet smell that has you rummaging through the kitchen cupboards looking for chips after your dog has had a good scratch sitting next to you.

As you might imagine, then, not just any bacteria can produce Frito Feet. Just as sodium and chloride ions bind to make salt, or cookies and cream combine to make, well, cookies 'n' cream, only bacteria from the Proteus and Pseudomonas families combine to make your dog's feet smell like Fritos. Both are very common. Proteus bacteria appear in decomposing animal matter and all those fun places where feces is found: intestines, manure, soil, and plants that have come in contact with animals. Proteus bacteria are known to cause urinary tract infections in both dogs and humans and tend to produce a sweet odor as they decompose.

Pseudomonas bacteria, on the other hand, are generally harmless to healthy humans but are often the culprit in nasty skin and ear infections in dogs. They are commonly found in water, soil, and plants all over the world and tend to smell more on the fruity side.[205] Together these two particular strains of bacteria cook up quite a corny treat in your dog's fuzzy feet. How's that for a song lyric?

Now, this isn't necessarily a bad thing, despite our tendency to worry any time Latin medical terms get thrown around about someone we love, including our four-legged family members. Dogs' paws are always going to smell, and to an extent this particular corn chip smell is as natural and normal as, say, your own BO, but if you want to keep it under control, you can commit to regular paw cleanings and to wiping down and drying off your dog's feet any time they go splish-splash through a muddy mudhole.

You should only be concerned about Frito Feet, veterinarians say, when either the smell or your dog's licking and

----

[205] *Pseudomonas aeruginosa*, which is among the most prevalent and most studied of the pseudomonas species, has been known to smell like grape juice when it infects burn patients.

ABOUT FRITOS

Fritos, which is the Spanish word for *fried* (this is relevant, give us a second), were "invented" by Charles Elmer Doolin in his mother's kitchen in San Antonio, Texas, in 1932. "Invented" is in quotes because it's probably more accurate to say Doolin white-labeled[206] them when he bought a corn chip business for $100 from a local soccer[207] coach named Gustavo Olguin, who was looking to return to Mexico, where he was from. The deal included Olguin's corn chip recipe, for which he used corn flour (called masa), the potato ricer he used to process the masa, and all his retail accounts—one of which, it seems likely, is where Doolin was first introduced to these delicious chips. Doolin was a hustler and a skilled salesman, and by the time he passed away in 1959, Fritos were everywhere, including Disneyland's own Mexican restaurant called Casa de Fritos.

Which has to make you wonder: Assuming dogs have had paws that smelled like corn chips since before the Great Depression, what did they call that smell before Fritos existed? As the chips spread across America, do you think when people opened their first bag they said, "Omigosh, these chips smell like my dog's feet!" Hey, maybe that's why Fritos are shaped like a dog's toenails!

---

[206] "White-labeling" is when a product or service allows the purchasing company to replace the branding with their own label. Ever seen those grocery-store knockoff cereals? That's it!

[207] Fútbol

chewing become excessive. That is often an indication of a bacterial infection—Funky Frito Feet, one might say—at which point it is probably time to bribe your dog into the back seat of the car with treats and take them on a ride for a date with the doctor and a personalized fitting for a cone of shame.

EVEN PUPPY'S BREATH IS CUTE

You can think of Frito Feet as perhaps something of an acquired taste among discerning dog lovers, but another smell associated with dogs—puppy breath—is, if we're daring to present opinion as fact in a book of facts, universally loved by every single human on Earth. Even cat people. Puppy breath is truly the stuff of legends. It's hard to accurately describe, as it's a smell unlike any other, so comparisons are kind of useless.[208] Regardless of its undefinability, people love it. But why exactly? Why do so many people love that smell so much?

Just like with Frito Feet, the answer lies with bacteria, though for the opposite reason. Whereas the presence of bacteria is what's responsible for the smell emanating from our dogs' feet, its absence is what appears to explain much about puppy breath's sweet smell.

It makes sense when you think about it. Puppies, by

---

[208] For the record, Chuck's wife, Emilie, always says it smells like toast. Many a stranger's puppies have been accosted while she yells, "Gimme some of that toast!" Confusion typically abounds.

virtue of their newness, have not yet had a chance to get into the bacteria-laden stuff that produces horrible breath in older dogs. Kind of like human babies. Filthy chew toys, bones, old shoes, sticks, chunks of kibble, hunks of poop. All the things that, if they aren't cleaned out from a dog's mouth sufficiently, create plaque, which makes bad breath, which sends our heads snapping back after one big whiff.

A PUPPY PSA IS NO SWEAT

A dog experiences a hot day differently than we do. It might feel nice out because there's a pleasant breeze, but that breeze is only pleasant to us because it's evaporating the sweat from the glands all over our bodies. Dogs don't have that luxury, however, because dogs don't sweat. They don't get the sweat-wicking experience of a cool breeze on a hot day; to them it's just hot out. Things can become even more dangerous for a dog when the heat combines with high humidity. The humidity prevents efficient heat transfer at their mouth through panting, which can set them up for heatstroke. What does all of this mean? Never exercise your dog in the heat of the afternoon, even when it feels nice out to you. Take them out quickly to do their business and then bring them back inside to resume their position on the kitchen floor or the bathroom floor. Start thinking like a dog and your dog will thank you for it.

In those first few months, puppies are basically pristine. The normal bacteria found in dog mouths stay relatively balanced as their baby teeth come in and then, a couple of months later, they start losing those tiny little razor blades as their adult teeth push through. At the same time, their guts haven't been altered either because their diets have consisted almost exclusively of their mother's milk.

Interestingly, some believe that it's wholly the mother's milk, that sweet life-giving nectar of the doggy gods, that explains puppy breath. But that sweet smell tends to persist past the weaning stage, so that can't be the whole answer. It's much more likely, according to what we've managed to cobble together from the vets who found time to write about this stuff, that all the changes going on in a puppy's body (mouth included) during its first six months of life, combined with limited exposure to plaque-producing pathogens, and of course mama's milk, explain why puppy kisses are the absolute best.

THE NOSE KNOWS

Interestingly, researchers have found that all the scents produced by bacteria, including Frito Feet and grown-up dog breath, don't just smell to us; they're "smelled" by bacteria as well. What we sense as a smell is, in other words, a chemical message that conveys some meaning and may produce a response. Poop smell, for example, generally carries the message that it comes from some kind of poopy pathogen and we should, therefore, move along and not play with said poop.

So long as an organism has some way to detect that chemical message, it may respond to it too. This extends to bacteria as well.

When fighting off antibiotics, bacteria often produce the chemical ammonia. Some recent research has found that through something called bacterial olfaction, other bacteria—even ones living a universe away (or, more precisely within entirely separate, but side-by-side, petri dishes)—sense the ammonia and respond to it as if it's a distress signal or a warning. They then throw up their shields by reducing what can move through their own cell membranes, which will prevent antibiotics from getting through.

The idea of bacterial olfaction is pretty neat, to be sure, but it pales in comparison to the astounding interestingness of dogs' ability to smell.

We've talked about dog olfaction in plenty of episodes, probably the most in-depth in our "How the Beagle Brigade Works" episode. But it's one of our favorite things to talk about, and this just wouldn't be a bona fide *Stuff You Should Know* book without some dog smell discussion.

Because dogs primarily navigate through the world with their highly attuned sense of smell, although an average-sized dog's brain is only 10 percent the size of a human's brain, the part responsible for processing smell is 40 times bigger. They have anywhere from 25 to 60 times more scent detectors than we do, which makes their sense of smell 10,000 to 100,000 times better than ours.[209] They even have a second olfactory system, called the vomeronasal organ (or

---

[209] Dogs have between 125 and 300 million scent receptors, depending on the breed. How that translates to a sense of smell that is 10,000 times stronger instead of 25 times (humans have a pitiful 5 to 6 million scent receptors), we have no idea, but them's the numbers.

Jacobson's organ), which allows them to pick up pheromones (remember, they are like perfume with a purpose). Then on top of all that, their noses are perpetually wet to make collecting scent particles easier, and they have horizontal slits on the bottom edge of each nostril to let them exhale out the sides without obstructing the inhale of fresh air (and scents) up the center. That's some serious double duty and gives them the ability to continually sniff, which is basically the canine version of circular breathing and just as cool.

And that's just dogs in general. We must also mention the scent hounds, whose big snouts and large nasal cavities make them the Dyson dual cyclone vacuum cleaners of smell collection. These are typically the breeds with big floppy ears (yes they are!) that help to sweep additional scent particles up toward their noses. They are exceptionally good at picking up scents in all kinds of environments: across flowing water; within large mounds of rubble; inside the human body (in the case of cancer-detecting dogs); even in gas tanks, as was the case with one drug-sniffing dog that found a bunch of marijuana submerged in a truck's full gas tank. Some can actually detect certain scents in parts per trillion, which, according to one dog cognition researcher, would be like detecting a half teaspoon of sugar in an Olympic-sized swimming pool.[210]

The top dog among all scent hounds is the bloodhound.

....

[210] This is akin to humans' own superability to detect a few parts per trillion of petrichor, the smell made just before it rains, like we talked about in our "Short Stuff" episode on that very subject.

This adorable, lumbering, wrinkly-skinned, droopy-faced pooch boasts up to 300 million scent receptors and is so reliable that evidence collected as a result of its tracking ability has been admitted in court.[211] That's not a joke. Like the basset hound, which is second in sniffing prowess, it also has a large flap of loose skin around its neck, called a "dewlap," that traps scent particles near its snout so it doesn't lose track of what it's trying to find.[212]

A CRIMINAL DEFENSE ATTORNEY'S GUIDE TO INDUCING A FALSE POSITIVE FROM THE WORLD'S BEST SCENT-DETECTING DOGS
(If the Crime Scene Is the Bedroom of a Filthy Teenage Boy)

SCENT RECEPTORS	DOG	BACTERIA FAMILY	WHAT WE SMELL
300 million	Blood-hound	Staphylo-coccus	Dirty sneakers
230 million	Basset hound	Nocardia	Musty basement

[211] Whether this should be the case is debatable. Dog-scenting evidence is considered by many to be junk science, perpetrated by nefarious handlers who subtly guide their dogs toward a conclusion that supports who they (or those who have hired them) think is guilty. You might say it's like phrenology of the nose.

[212] When he was a kid, Chuck had a basset hound whose ears were so big the dog would step on them while walking.

SCENT RECEPTORS	DOG	BACTERIA FAMILY	WHAT WE SMELL
225 million	Beagle	Candida	Yeast
125 million	Dachs-hund	Hae-mophilus	Wet fur
5 million	The Bounty Hunter	Coryne-bacterium	Fruit

Sense of smell is not the only place where dogs show exceptional ability above and beyond human beings, though it is definitely the most impressive. Dogs can see better in low light, like at sunrise and sunset, and they can track moving objects much better. They can hear much better too, even though they're born deaf and stay that way for about their first month of life. Once mature, however, they can hear four times as far as the average human and at a much higher pitch as well. None of which seems to make one bit of difference when you yell at them to get their paws out of your face after they've woken you up from the most delicious dream about Frito pie.

CHAPTER 14

~~~~~~

CHILD PRODIGIES

PRECOCIOUS MIMICS OR TINY GENIUSES?

In a perfect world, every discussion of child prodigies would begin with the quirky 2001 movie *The Royal Tenenbaums* and its three kid geniuses.

There's Chas, the brilliant business mind; Margot, the award-winning playwright; and Richie, the tennis phenom. Sadly, these siblings are fictional characters, so a real conversation about prodigies should probably start with Wolfgang Amadeus Mozart.

Little Wolfie began playing the harpsichord at three years old, when most kids are just learning to wipe their own behinds (if they are lucky). By five, he was writing music. By seven, he was touring with his older sister, Maria Anna.[213] By

....

[213] Many historians believe Maria Anna was nearly as talented as her younger brother, if not equally so, but once she reached "marrying age" in 1769, her father pulled her from the tour. She had to stay home in Salzburg, Austria (probably practicing her sewing), while her little brother trotted across Europe, playing all of their favorite songs.

his teenage years, he'd written numerous concertos and symphonies that are still being performed today—that's over 250 years and still going strong! Along with the Spanish painter Pablo Picasso, who could draw before he could talk, and the mysterious American chess world champion Bobby Fischer, who became a grandmaster at fifteen years old, Mozart is considered the epitome of the child prodigy.

But when you dig into the history of child prodigies, what you realize is that these great historical figures are anything but typical. They are the exceptions to the exceptional.

WHAT IS A PRODIGY?

In America at least, nowhere is the race to keep up with the Joneses more pronounced than in the competition between parents to prove how advanced their children are.

DIEGO KNEW HIS ABCS BY THE TIME HE STARTED PRESCHOOL.

MY MADISON READ THE ENTIRE HARRY POTTER SERIES BY THE TIME SHE WAS SIX.

OUR LITTLE JAYLA READ BAUDELAIRE IN FRENCH WHEN SHE WAS FIVE.

You know those parents. But these hypothetical advanced children would never be considered prodigies—sorry, parents!—because it isn't about being ahead of your peers: It's about not having any peers at all. To be a child prodigy is to meaningfully display talent or ability before the teen years that meets or exceeds adult levels of expertise.

That is the main difference between proficiency and prodigy. Prodigies are doing something as kids that most adults couldn't do. And yet that only touches on the output of the prodigy—it doesn't get to the heart of what makes one.

According to experts, child prodigies possess a few distinguishing characteristics: They have incredible working memories; they have exceptional focus and attention to detail; and they have what Boston College psychology professor Ellen Winner calls a "rage to master," which is sort of like a combo of obsession and perfectionism. It's also a great album title. Together, these traits allow a child prodigy to hold large, complex concepts in their mind, break them down into their component parts, and work on each piece nonstop until the whole thing is perfect.

Like Priyanshi Somani, from Gujarat, India, who won the Mental Calculation World Cup as an eleven-year-old by solving for the square roots of ten six-digit numbers in less than seven minutes. No big deal.

Or like Taylor Wilson, who built a bomb at the age of ten and a nuclear fusor as a fourteen-year-old,[214] then designed an underground molten salt reactor (a nuclear device to generate energy while using up nuclear waste) that he presented at the TED Conference in 2013 as a nineteen-year-old. Whew!

....

[214] A fusor is a device that creates nuclear fusion. The most common type was invented by Philo T. Farnsworth, who is most famous for having invented the electric television—a design he came up with at almost the exact same age as Wilson when he made his fusor.

For many kids like Somani and Wilson, the pursuit of excellence and expertise becomes all-consuming. They will forgo nearly everything that interests other kids their age—playing video games, watching TV—in order to spend more time engaging with their obsession. Parents of prodigies report having to drag their children away from their keyboards, their musical instruments, their workbenches, just to make sure they do the most basic things, like eat or bathe or go to school.

WHAT MAKES A PRODIGY?

Very little is understood about the biological basis of prodigies, but it appears that the cerebellum plays a big role in making a prodigy possible. Rhyming with antebellum (like those old southern plantations), the cerebellum is one of two *c*'s in the brain. The other *c* is the cerebrum. If the brain was like a mullet haircut, the cerebrum would be the business in the front and the cerebellum would be the party in the rear.

Located in the hindbrain—at the bottom, connected to the brain stem—the cerebellum makes up only 10 percent of the brain's overall size[215] but contains 50 percent of its total neurons, which means there's a lot going on back there. Typically, we've thought of it as being responsible for fine

---

[215] In Latin, cerebellum means "little brain."

motor skills (like writing, texting, using a joystick) and for coordinating movements that are controlled by that other c, which is also responsible for intelligence and memory.

But research in recent decades has shown that the cerebellum doesn't just coordinate physical movement; it coordinates thinking processes as well. It has evolved that way over the last million years or so, during which time the cerebellum has tripled in size and developed intricate circuit-type connections to the cerebrum. These connections have allowed the cerebellum to improve skills that reside in the cerebrum. Think of it as a gamer named Cerebellum, who can jump into Cerebrum's character. She's got full use of Cerebrum's weapons, shields, snot rags, you name it. She can even add to Cerebrum's health points, but to get any good, she's got to practice.

This brings up the age-old "nature versus nurture" argument. Are child prodigies born or made? If obsession and focus and practice are essential elements of prodigy behavior, then surely prodigies are made, right? It's true that Mozart played music three hours a day from the time he was very young; that Picasso drew and painted and sketched and sculpted incessantly; that Tiger Woods was at the course with his father, Earl, every day; that the Williams sisters practiced multiple hours every day for their entire childhoods. But none of that explains why Picasso's first word was *pencil*, or how Tiger Woods could hit an entire bucket of golf balls at eighteen months old, or how Mozart played the harpsichord at three, or how Venus and Serena Williams gravitated to tennis as four-year-olds.

Clearly, as it is every time the nature versus nurture question gets raised, the answer is both. Child prodigies are naturally gifted and naturally interested children who are nurtured by parents, mentors, and coaches to indulge their obsessions and to practice as much as they need to in order to get better and achieve whatever goals they have set for themselves. Some parents will homeschool their kids to give them more practice time; others will move their entire family so their kids can be around the best. Richard Williams did both. He homeschooled Venus and Serena until they went to high school, and he moved them from California to Florida when Venus was ten and Serena was nine so they could train at a prestigious tennis academy.

That said, to the extent that you can help to make a child prodigy, you can also break one. For every Tiger Woods there is a Todd Marinovich. For every Venus and Serena Williams there is a Jennifer Capriati. Both Marinovich and Capriati were considered prodigies in their respective sports—football and tennis—as young kids, and were pushed, some would say bullied, by overbearing fathers until they washed out or burned out. Both had much shorter careers than anyone expected; both had trouble with drugs and run-ins with the law during and after their playing days. Any talent or interest that Marinovich and Capriati had for their sports was seemingly corrupted by the self-interest of parents who pushed their kids to practice more in pursuit of their own goals rather than their kids'.

IT'S HARD OUT HERE FOR A KID

The struggle for child prodigies begins much earlier than adulthood. It starts in childhood with making friends. While most prodigies don't mind being alone and often enjoy spending long hours by themselves perfecting their talents, eventually everyone wants a friend. When you're a young kid, friendships are based on simple things you have in common with the people around you. But if you're not around many people, and you're most interested in nuclear fusion or mastering Beethoven's "Hammerklavier,"[216] the pickings for friends are going to be slim.

The real test for child prodigies, though—perhaps the only one they will ever struggle to pass—is when they age out of

---

[216] Composed between 1817 and 1818, the sonata is considered Beethoven's most technically difficult piece of music to perform.

the prodigy label. "Most prodigies do not make the leap in early adulthood from mastery to major creative discoveries," Ellen Winner said. That's the real reason why the conversation around child prodigies should begin with *The Royal Tenenbaums* and not Mozart or Picasso or Bobby Fischer. The Tenenbaum kids turned into a collective mess, which is far more common for child prodigies than great wealth or acclaim. Mozart and Picasso and Fischer, on the other hand, managed to revolutionize music, painting, and chess. Drop the mic.

For normal prodigies, it's the jump from kid genius to adult genius that's so hard. For years, child prodigies are at the top of their game, chased by the paparazzi, exalted for doing things at an adult level of expertise. Except it's in a field of study that already exists. And then, when they grow up and cannot rocket beyond that, by definition they cease to be all that special. They get jobs, and they become more or less just like everyone around them. They have peers; they are no longer peerless.

To be fair, most child prodigies don't fall off a cliff or become a mess like those fictional Tenenbaums. They lead fairly normal, productive lives, working successfully in fields they've had a lifelong talent in and passion for. And there are worse fates to befall young geniuses, let's be clear. They could end up hosting a podcast about stuff you should know and wake up every morning asking themselves the same question: "I memorized all those Trivial Pursuit cards as a kid for THIS?" No one in their right mind would want that life!

STUFF YOU SHOULD KNOW
PODCAST EPISODES

A decade-plus of researching and talking about anything and everything that has piqued our interest informs so much of what has gone into this book. That fact is in evidence here in the podcast episode appendix, which is, functionally speaking, an audio bibliography (the title we considered assigning to this section if it were not both so fancy and so schmancy). These podcasts, and all the rest, are available at www.iheart.com/podcast.

MR. POTATO HEAD: AMERICA'S TOY
- "A Partial History of Action Figures" (November 3, 2016); "Etch A Sketch!" (March 28, 2019); "How Silly Putty Works" (October 4, 2011); "How Play-Doh Works" (August 5, 2014); "How Slinky Works" (April 14, 2015); "How Barbie® Doll Works" (December 20, 2012); "The Rubik's Cube Episode" (August 29, 2019); "How Easy-Bake Ovens Work" (November 1, 2018); and "E.T.: Is It Really the Worst Video Game of All Time?" (December 20, 2018)
- "How We Almost Got Rid of Polio" (July 21, 2020)

HOW TO GET LOST: AND SEVEN WAYS TO STAY LIKE THAT
- "How Search and Rescue Works" (August 7, 2018); "How Search and Rescue Dogs Work" (December 4, 2018)

DEMOLITION DERBIES: WHY WE LOVE TO WATCH THINGS GO BOOM!

- "How Crime Scene Photography Works" (February 17, 2011)
- "The Gettysburg Address: Short and Sweet" (July 14, 2016); "Evel Knievel Part I" (August 9, 2016) and "Evel Knievel Part II" (August 11, 2016)

FACIAL HAIR: THE LONG AND SHORT OF IT

- "What's the deal with duckbill platypuses?" (April 9, 2013)
- "Body Odor: You Stink" (April 11, 2012)
- "Vocal Fry and Other Speech Trends" (October 22, 2015)

BACKMASKING: WHEN RECORDING BACKWARD IS MOVING FORWARD

- "Was the PMRC censorship in disguise?" (December 6, 2018)
- "Little, Fluffy Clouds" (January 11, 2011); "Shroud of Turin: No Ordinary Bed Sheet" (March 30, 2017)

AGING: DO WE GOTTA?

- "Dr. Elizabeth Blackwell, Feminist Physician" (April 9, 2020); "The Great Stink: The Stench So Bad They Gave It a Name" (March 14, 2009); "Frances Perkins: Influential and Unknown" (September 8, 2020)
- "10 Accidental Inventions: By the Numbers" (June 21, 2012); "How did Nikola Tesla change the way we use energy?" (June 9, 2009); "SYSK Live: The Kellogg Brothers' Wacky World of Health" (January 22, 2019)
- "How HeLa Cells Work" (December 10, 2013) and "Does the body replace itself?" (March 31, 2015)
- "Can your grandfather's diet shorten your life?" (June 10, 2010)

THE PET ROCK: THE SAVIOR OF 1975 (OR THE DUMBEST TOY OF THE BEST DECADE)

- "We Are Running Out of Sand and That Actually Matters" (September 24, 2019)

- "SYSK Live: Back When Ford Pintos Were Flaming Deathtraps" (March 1, 2018); "How Disco Works" (July 17, 2012); "How the Amityville Horror Worked" (October 25, 2018)

DO(UGH)NUTS: THE HISTORY OF AMERICA'S SNACK FOOD
- "Coffee: The World's Drug of Choice" (December 29, 2011)
- "Is yogurt a miracle food?" (November 8, 2018)

THE JERSEY DEVIL: HOO IS THE MONSTER OF THE PINE BARRENS
- "How Soccer Works" (June 19, 2014)
- "How Friday the 13th Works" (February 12, 2009)

TRILLIONAIRES: ARE THEY POSSIBLE, AND WHO WILL IT BE?
- "How Currency Works" (September 18, 2014); "How much money is in the world?" (September 5, 2013); and "What is stagflation?" (February 24, 2011)
- "What was the KGB?" (July 7, 2020)
- "How AI Facial Recognition Works" (February 4, 2020)

THE SCOTLAND YARD CRIME MUSEUM: NOTHING TO SEE HERE
- "How Death Masks Work" (January 15, 2013); "How Fingerprinting Works" (August 1, 2013); "How Champagne Works" (May 16, 2017) and "How the Great Train Robbery Worked" (October 16, 2014); "5 Successful Counterfeiters" (May 13, 2010) and "How Spies Work" (February 23, 2013)
- "Sir Isaac Newton: Greatest Scientist of All Time?" (January 19, 2016)
- "How did language evolve?" (May 1, 2012); "Why does music provoke emotion?" (September 20, 2012)

WELL-WITCHING: THE ANCIENT ART OF GUESSING WITH A STICK

- "Animal Migration: Where's that gnu gnoing?" (November 2, 2010); "Elephants: The Best Animals?" (February 14, 2019)
- "How Gold Works" (January 31, 2013); "Cleopatra: Ms. Understood" (July 9, 2019); "How Project Star Gate Worked" (June 9, 2020)
- "How Ouija Boards Work" (October 29, 2013)
- "How Morphic Fields Work" (March 3, 2020); "How the Scientific Method Works" (January 13, 2015)
- "How Occam's Razor Works" (May 24, 2018)

DOG SMELLS: CANINE SCENTS AND SENSE-ABILITY

- "How Roller Coasters Work, Minus the Fun" (April 28, 2011)
- "Oh Yes, How Soil Works" (July 2, 2020)
- "How the Beagle Brigade Works" (June 13, 2017)
- "Do animals have a sixth sense?" (May 21, 2009); "How Marijuana Works" (May 1, 2014)
- "Short Stuff: Petrichor" (August 14, 2019)
- "Prisons: Not as Fun as You'd Think" (August 12, 2010)

CHILD PRODIGIES: PRECOCIOUS MIMICS OR TINY GENIUSES?

- "Short Stuff: Mullets: 'Nuff Said" (April 29, 2020)

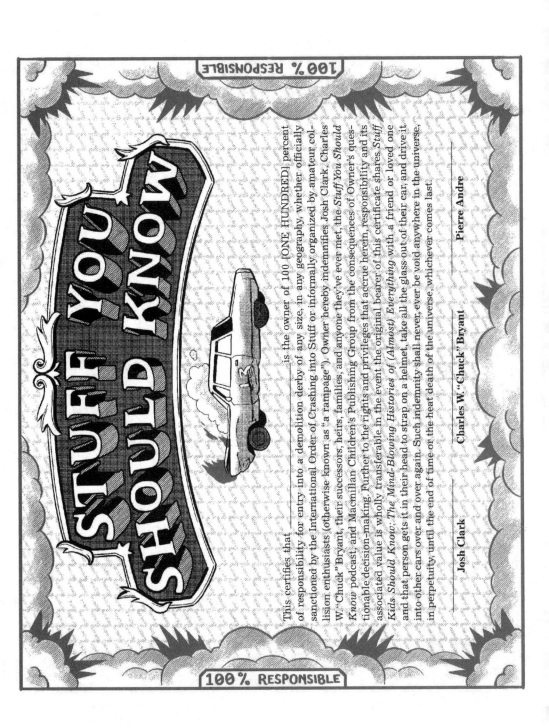

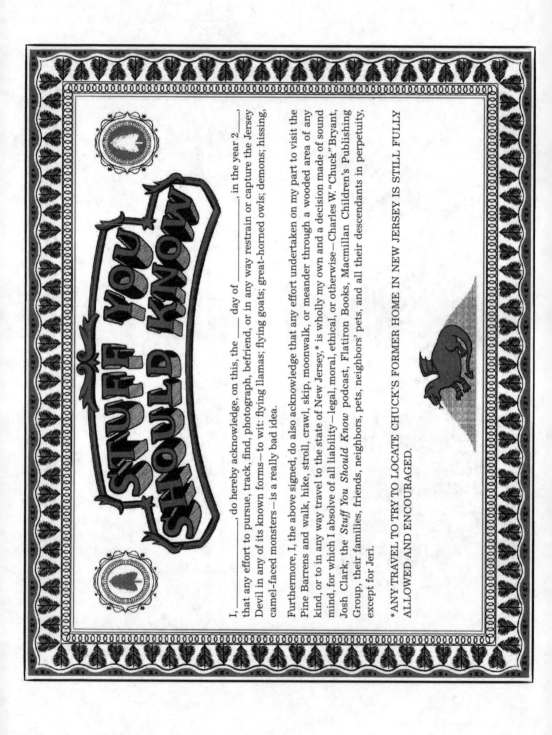

I, _____, do hereby acknowledge, on this, the ____ day of _____, in the year 2____, that any effort to pursue, track, find, photograph, befriend, or in any way restrain or capture the Jersey Devil in any of its known forms—to wit: flying llamas; flying goats; great-horned owls; demons; hissing, camel-faced monsters—is a really bad idea.

Furthermore, I, the above signed, do also acknowledge that any effort undertaken on my part to visit the Pine Barrens and walk, hike, stroll, crawl, skip, moonwalk, or meander through a wooded area of any kind, or to in any way travel to the state of New Jersey,* is wholly my own and a decision made of sound mind, for which I absolve of all liability—legal, moral, ethical, or otherwise—Charles W. "Chuck" Bryant, Josh Clark, the *Stuff You Should Know* podcast, Flatiron Books, Macmillan Children's Publishing Group, their families, friends, neighbors, pets, neighbors' pets, and all their descendants in perpetuity, except for Jeri.

*ANY TRAVEL TO TRY TO LOCATE CHUCK'S FORMER HOME IN NEW JERSEY IS STILL FULLY ALLOWED AND ENCOURAGED.

STUFF YOU SHOULD KNOW

DATE

ABOUT THE AUTHOR

JOSH CLARK

Josh Clark has been writing since childhood, but the adult edition of this book, *Stuff You Should Know: An Incomplete Compendium*, is his first book. In 2008, he transitioned from writing for a living to speaking when he started making podcasts, including *SYSK, SKSK*, and his ten-part series *The End of the World*. He's enjoyed getting back to writing.

When he's not working, Josh likes to do things that have nothing to do with deadlines or computers—riding bikes with his wife, Umi, and their daughter with four legs, Momo; working outdoors; and digging and chopping and the like.

Josh's home is wherever Umi and Momo are, mostly between Florida's Space Coast and Atlanta.

ABOUT THE AUTHOR
CHUCK BRYANT

Chuck never imagined he'd make his career as a professional talker and imitation comedian. He figured he'd be a teacher, and weirdly, he's also that. In addition to *SYSK* and *SKSK*, he hosts his beloved *Movie Crush* and works in podcast development.

At home in Atlanta, he hangs out with his wife, Emilie; daughter, Ruby; and their cats and dogs, mostly laughing and being as silly as possible. He also plays guitar and sings in his old-man band, El Cheapo, with his dear friends Eddie, Jim, and Chris, at various neighborhood festivals and basements.

ABOUT
iHeartMedia

iHeartMedia is the number-one audio company in the United States, reaching nine out of ten Americans every month—and with a quarter of a billion monthly listeners, it has a greater reach than any other media company in the United States. The company's leading position in audio extends across multiple platforms, including more than 850 live broadcast stations in over 160 markets nationwide; its iHeartRadio digital service, available across more than 250 platforms and 2,000 devices; its influencers; social media; branded iconic live music events; other digital products and newsletters; and podcasts as the number-one commercial podcast publisher. iHeartMedia also leads the audio industry in analytics, targeting, and attribution for its marketing partners with its SmartAudio product, using data from its massive consumer base. Visit iHeartMedia.com for more company information.

WORKS CITED FOR YOUNG READER'S EDITION

"Biographical Overview | C. Everett Koop—Profiles in Science." *U.S. National Library of Medicine*, National Institutes of Health, profiles.nlm.nih.gov/spotlight/qq/feature/biographical-overview.

Borowski, Susan. "The Origin and Popular Use of Occam's Razor." *American Association for the Advancement of Science*, June 12, 2012, https://www.aaas.org/origin-and-popular-use-occams-razor.

"Destruction Derby." IMDb.com, imdb.com/title/tt1988596/.

Duck Soup Producktions. "Mr. Potato Head Saves Veggie Valley." *Internet Archive*, January 1, 1995, archive.org/details/mr-potato-head-saves-veggie-valley.

Eschner, Kat. "John D. Rockefeller Was the Richest Person to Ever Live. Period." *Smithsonian Magazine*, January 10, 2017, smithsonianmag.com/smart-news/john-d-rockefeller-richest-person-ever-live-period-180961705/.

Greenemeier, Larry. "U.S. and Soviet Spooks Studied Paranormal Powers to Find a Cold War Advantage." *Scientific American Blog Network*, October 29, 2008, blogs.scientificamerican.com/news-blog/us-and-soviet-spooks-studied-parano-2008-10-29/.

Harding, Luke. "Vladimir Putin Hugs Polar Bear on Arctic Trip." *The Guardian*, April 29, 2010, theguardian.com /world/2010/apr/29/vladimir-putin-polar-bear-arctic.

Hasbro. "Mr. Potato Head Brand Update." Posted February 25, 2021. corporate.hasbro.com/en-us/articles/create_your _potato_head_family_launching_this_fall.

"The History Blog." *The History Blog RSS*, December 27, 2014, thehistoryblog.com/page/274?qHe.

Hill, Kenneth. *Lost Person Behaviour*. Ottawa: National SAR Secretariat. 1999.

Honeycombe, Gordon. *Dark Secrets of the Black Museum: 1835–1985: More Dark Secrets from 150 Years of the Most Notorious Crimes in England*. London: John Blake, 2014.

"How a Giant Python Swallowed an Indonesian Woman." *BBC News*, June 18, 2018, bbc.com/news/world-asia -39427462.

Imperial College London. "New Insights into Skin Cells Could Explain Why Our Skin Doesn't Leak." *Science-Daily*, November 29, 2016, sciencedaily.com/releases /2016/11/161129114910.htm.

Jenkins, Eileen K., Mallory T. DeChant, and Erin B. Perry. "When the Nose Doesn't Know: Canine Olfactory Function Associated with Health, Management, and Potential Links to Microbiota." *Frontiers in Veterinary Science* 5 (March 29, 2018). doi.org/10.3389/fvets.2018.00056. Accessed July 13, 2022.

Kempire Radio. "Claude Kelly Gives The Stories Behind Britney Spears 'Circus', Fantasia's 'Bittersweet' & Others." September 1, 2011. youtube.com/watch?v=5TttfWnScoM. Accessed August 20, 2022.

Koester, Robert J. *Lost Person Behavior: a Search and Rescue Guide on Where to Look—For Land, Air, and Water*. Charlottesville: dbS Productions LLC. 2008.

Le Piane, Krista. "The Evolution of Quiet Flight in Owls (Strigiformes) and Lesser Nighthawks (Chodeiles acutipennis." PhD Diss., University of California Riverside, December 2020. escholarship.org/uc/item/2b35r9pd. Accessed July 7, 2022.

López-Otín, Carlos., Maria A. Blasco, Linda Partridge, Manuel Serrano, and Guido Kroemer. "The Hallmarks of Aging." *Cell* 153, issue 6 (June 6, 2013): 1194-1217. https://doi.org/10.1016/j.cell.2013.05.039.

"The Longest Note Record Gets Broken, or Maybe Not." *NPR*, May 11, 2017, npr.org/2017/05/11/527895011/the -longest-note-record-gets-broken-or-maybe-not.

Maire, Louis F., and Major J.D. LaMothe. *Soviet and Czechoslovakian Parapsychology Research: The DIA Report from 1975 with New Addenda*. Lulu.com, 2014.

Maurer, M., M. Rietzler, R. Burghardt, and F. Siebenhaar. "The Male Beard Hair and Facial Skin—Challenges for Shaving." *International Journal of Cosmetic Science* 38, no. 51 (May 22, 2016): 3–9. doi.org/10.1111/ics.12328.

Michals, Debra. "Elizabeth Blackwell." National Women's History Museum, 2015, womenshistory.org/education -resources/biographies/elizabeth-blackwell.

Morris, Evan. "Cop." *The Word Detective*, December 8, 2014, word-detective.com/2014/12/cop-2/.

Nix, Elizabeth. "Why Were American Soldiers in WWI Called Doughboys?" *History.com*, September 28, 2018, https://

www.history.com/news/why-were-americans-who
-served-in-world-war-i-called-doughboys.

Perez, Matt. "Top-Earning Video Gamers: The Ten Highest-
Paid Players Pocketed More than $120 Million in 2019."
Forbes, January 29, 2020, forbes.com/sites/mattperez
/2020/01/29/top-earning-video-gamers-the-ten-highest
-paid-players-pocketed-more-than-120-million-in-2019
/?sh=46ed81e4880b.

"Plants of the Pine Barrens Ecosystem." Pinelands Pres-
ervation Alliance, pinelandsalliance.org/learn-about
-the-pinelands/ecosystem/pinelands-plants-overview
/plants-of-the-pine-barrens.

Rochford, Caroline. *Great Victorian Inventions: Novel Con-
trivances and Industrial Revolutions*. Stroud, Gloucester-
shire: Amberley Publishing, 2014.

Roland, Elisa. "46 Etiquette Tips of the Victorian Era That
Need to Make a Comeback." *Reader's Digest*, February 4,
2022, rd.com/list/victorian-era-etiquette/.

"Russia's Putin Admits Wildlife Stunts Are Staged." *BBC
News*, September 13, 2012, bbc.com/news/world-europe
-19591179.

"Senator Ted Kennedy Drives Car off Bridge at Chap-
paquiddick Island." *History.com*, February 9, 2010, history
.com/this-day-in-history/incident-on-chappaquiddick
-island.

Thitaram, Chatchote, Nikorn Thongtip, Chaleamchart
Somgird, Ben Colenbrander, Dick C. J. van Boxtel, Frank
van Steenbeek, and Johannes A. Lenstra. "Evaluation and
Selection of Microsatellite Markers for an Identification

and Parentage Test of Asian Elephants (Elephas Maximus)." *Conservation Genetics* 9, no. 4 (August 29, 2007): 921–925. doi.org/10.1007/s10592-007-9406-z. Accessed July 8, 2022.

"Tobacco-Related Mortality." Centers for Disease Control and Prevention, April 28, 2020, cdc.gov/tobacco/data _statistics/fact_sheets/health_effects/tobacco_related _mortality/index.htm.

"Top Names of the 1950s." Social Security Administration. ssa.gov/oact/babynames/decades/names1950s.html.

Valinsky, Jordan. "The CEO behind Fortnite Makes It to the Forbes 400 List." *CNN Business*, October 2, 2019, cnn.com/2019/10/02/business/forbes-400-billionaire -list-trnd/index.html.

"Why Are We Involved." Centers for Disease Control and Prevention, October 8, 2021, cdc.gov/polio/why-are-we -involved/index.htm.

Wilde, Megan. "The Evolution of Mr. Potato Head." *Mental Floss*, March 11, 2022, mentalfloss.com/article/27105 /putting-good-face-it-evolution-mr-potato-head.